DISCERNING GOD'S WILL
Together

Published in association with the Eastern Mennonite Seminary School for Leadership Training and Mennonite Church USA

The Living Issues Discussion Series

*T*HE LIVING ISSUES DISCUSSION SERIES is edited by Michael A. King and published by Cascadia Publishing House (earlier by Pandora Press U.S.) as well as sometimes copublished with Herald Press. Cascadia Publishing House, in consultation with its Editorial Council as well as volume editors and authors, is primarily responsible for content of these studies. Tpically through a main text followed by materials providing affirming and critical reactions from respondents, these volumes address "living issues" likely to benefit from lively and serious discussion.

1. To Continue the Dialogue:
   Biblical Interpretation and Homosexuality
   Edited by C. Norman Kraus, 2001

2. What Does the Bible Really Say About Hell?
   Wrestling with the Traditional View
   By Randy Klassen, 2001

3. Reflecting on Faith in a Post-Christian Time (a revised and expanded edition of Theology in Postliberal Perspective, first published by SCM Press and Trinity Press International)
   By Daniel Liechty, 2003

4. Stumbling Toward a Genuine Conversation on Homosexuality
   Edited by Michael A. King, 2007

5. Theology as if Jesus Matters:
   An Introduction to Christianity's Main Themes
   Ted Grimsrud, 2009

6. Rethinking Religion:
   Beyond Scientism, Theism, and Philosophic Doubt
   Alan Soffin, 2011

7. Discerning God's Will Together:
   Biblical Interpretation in the Free Church Tradition
   Ervin R. Stutzman, 2013

DISCERNING GOD'S WILL
Together

Biblical Interpretation
in the
Free Church Tradition

ERVIN R. STUTZMAN

Foreword by
Sara Wenger Shenk
Responses by
David Brubaker, Sally Weaver Glick, Jan Wood

Living Issues Discussion Series Volume 7

Publishing House
Telford, Pennsylvania

Cascadia Publishing House LLC orders, information, reprint permissions:
contact@cascadiapublishinghouse.com
1-215-723-9125
126 Klingerman Road, Telford PA 18969
www.CascadiaPublishingHouse.com

Discerning God's Will Together
Copyright © 2013 by Cascadia Publishing House
a division of Cascadia Publishing House LLC, Telford, PA 18969
Library of Congress Catalog Number: 2013000012
ISBN 13: 978-1-931038-95-9; **ISBN 10:** 1-931038-95-3
Book design by Cascadia Publishing House
Cover design by Dawn Ranck

The paper used in this publication is recycled and meets the
minimum requirements of American National Standard for Information Sciences—Permanence of Paper for Printed Library Materials, ANSI
Z39.48-1984.

Library of Congress Cataloguing-in-Publication Data
Stutzman, Ervin R., 1953-
[Biblical interpretation in the Free Church]
Discerning God's will together : biblical interpretation in the Free Church
tradition / Ervin R. Stutzman.
  pages cm. -- (Living issues discussion series ; 7)
Includes bibliographical references.
Summary: "This book invites congregations to learn communal forms of
biblical interpretation through which to implement practices of discernment offering guidance amid today's perplexing moral problems"--Pro-
vided by publisher.
ISBN 978-1-931038-95-9 (5. 5 x 8.5" trade pbk. : alk. paper) -- ISBN 1-
931038-95-3 (5. 5 x 8.5" trade pbk. : alk. paper)
1. Discernment (Christian theology) 2. Bible--Criticism, interpretation,
etc. 3. Church group work. 4. Mennonite Church USA--Doctrines. 5. An-
abaptists--Doctrines. I. Title.

BV4509.5.S854 2013
230'.97--dc23

2013000012

18 17 16 15 13   10 9 8 7 6 5 4 3 2 1

I appeal to you therefore, brothers and sisters,
by the mercies of God, to present your bodies as a living
sacrifice, holy and acceptable to God, which is your spiritual
worship. Do not be conformed to this world, but be
transformed by the renewing of your minds, so that
you may discern what is the will of God—what is
good and acceptable and perfect.
—Romans 12:1-2 NRSV

Contents

....

Foreword

*H*OW TIMELY IT IS In the hurly burly fractiousness of our times for Ervin Stutzman (and publisher Michael A. King) to lift up the core practice of discernment for all to consider afresh. What could be more renewing for the church than to reclaim the long held Anabaptist Mennonite ideal of "corporate discernment and action under the leading of the Holy Spirit"? I can't imagine anything more important than to gather as two or three (at least)—in Jesus' name. That's where Jesus has promised to meet us.

Stutzman cites authors who observe that communal discernment has often not worked well for heirs of the Anabaptists. Yet despite many failures, we continue to hold up this glowing vision because we believe that we're really onto something. We tenaciously believe that to seek a common mind within a shared conversation (for the purpose of a more unified witness) is not only a worthy goal—but the very heartbeat of God's reconciling mission in the world.

Stutzman's survey of Mennonite perspectives on discernment seems largely meant to serve communities that many of us who are aging, white, Swiss Germans grew up with. We generally learned to regard difference as a problem. Many times I've heard the comment about an event in these mostly homogeneous communities: "Well, it was different alright." Stutzman's move to normalize difference with a discussion of paradoxical truths embedded even in Scripture may seem radical for those who live in somewhat isolated communities of sameness. It rings true for communities who embrace many cultures and perspectives as the multi-splendored ways God is made known to us.

Holding together point-and-counterpoint as contrasting frames of reference helps me better see what is captured within any particular frame. That's surely the case with *Discerning God's Will Together*.

A counterpoint for me while reading this manuscript was watching the birds on a sun-bathed, snow white morning. I counted at least eighteen varieties of feathered beauties negotiating space at the feeder. At times the large flickers, blue jays, and red-bellied woodpeckers chased other birds away. Most of the time, the smaller chickadees, juncos, sparrows, wrens, nuthatches, tufted titmice, downy woodpeckers, doves, blue birds, and finches feasted side by side with relative equanimity. There is plenty of food so no bird goes hungry, but negotiating access to the vital seed is a dynamic, fluctuating tension.

To teach his followers about trust, Jesus changed his frame of reference. He invited his worried listeners to "Look at the birds of the air. . . . " He reminded his fearful disciples that while the market values two sparrows at just a penny, "not one of them will fall to the ground apart from your Father. . . . So do not be afraid."

Stutzman is a master craftsman. He skillfully frames discernment as the function of responsible discipleship. He is familiar with good process so vital for bringing order out of chaos. I value this organizational approach to churchly matters. I also keep listening for the music of the Spirit. For the wild, in-breaking of revelation. For humbling conviction that moves us to our knees and heartfelt testimony that breaks open our givens. It is the dumbfounding aha! of discernment that I long for—and am thus drawn with Jesus to consider the birds.

Discernment is more than five steps for managing conflict, as important as that is. Beyond dutiful diligence, how might listening for what "the heavens are telling" awaken insight? How might discerning practices for life abundant become the heartbeat of a community of shalom—a community to which persons will flock, as did the Anabaptists and the early church, to meet Jesus?

What I found most moving about Stutzman's overview is the acknowledgement that reconciliation lies at the heart of the Christian message and that often the path to reconciliation is paved with pain—yes, even the pain of conflict. Anabaptist Mennonite Biblical Seminary New Testament professor Mary Schertz writes that taking the cross of Jesus seriously means that suffering love is to be played out in the arena of discernment around difficult issues, as in all other areas of our common life. There can be no holier, compassionate work than to understand each other and God better by engaging in the difficult conversations that we currently find ourselves amid.

By staying in fellowship with each other through the humbling, hard, and joyous work of discernment we will come to know how awesome is the love of Christ "who for the sake of the joy that was set before him endured the cross." Our hearts will be tugged (painfully) wider and wider open as we hold together in love what seems irreconcilable—giving thanks for a Lord in whom "all things hold together" and through whom "God was pleased to reconcile to himself all things."

—*Sara Wenger Shenk, Elkhart, Indiana*
 President, Anabaptist Mennonite Biblical Seminary

·······················

Series Editor's Preface

*I*N TODAY'S EVER MORE POLARIZED WORLD, the aim of the Living
Issues Discussion Series is to showcase Cascadia authors able
to bridge conflictual stances. To set conversation in motion,
typically books in the series include a vigorous statement of
position regarding issues sometimes controversial in faith cir-
cles. Then, after a book's main text, a Responses chapter provides affirming and critical commentary.

Setting Living Issues books in the context of responses is
important to the series goals in that we at least dream of responses as helping to place the book in the midst of mutually
respectful discussion within which a) all perspectives are seen
as fallible and open to enlargement through respectful critique
and at the same time b) all are seen as potential treasures from
which even opposing viewpoints can benefit.

Discerning God's Will Together differs from other series en-
tries that focus on intrinsically controversial issues. In contrast,
Ervin Stutzman intends less to comment on given topics and
more to guide the discerning community through discernment-
centered biblical interpretation as it navigates difficult issues.
Thus respondents affirm ways Stutzman has succeeded in providing such a resource and suggest ways the book can benefit
from their views of how the church might address complex discernment matters.

This has led to valuable feedback from respondents, each in some way involved in exploring discernment processes as resources for navigating divisive agenda. Jan Wood, author (with Bruce Bishop and Lon Fendall) of *Practicing Discernment Together*, sees Stutzman as providing "a rich treasure trove of insights and information" and also still yearns for another resource on the "personal discipleship/faithfulness required to prepare and empower folks to be helpful participants in healthy congregational life and discernment." Responding through her foreword, Sara Wenger Shenk joins Wood in "listening for the music of the Spirit" as through discernment we form "a community to which persons will flock. . . ."

Sally Weaver Glick, author of *In Tune with God*, notes how vital it is for the discipleship in which discernment is grounded to be a response to God's grace and that talk of "God's will" can be off-putting to some. She invites discernment to unfold within celebration of "all that gives God delight and is in line with God's purposes, all that is in tune with God's song."

David Brubaker, who works with discernment agenda as Associate Professor Organizational Studies at the Center for Justice and Peacebuilding of Eastern Mennonite University, underscores that "congregations matter." He believes that amid the schismatic forces of our era, discernment must prioritize the local community and requires "not only the theology and tools that Stutzman carefully develops but also a firm rejection of Constantinian models of monolithic decision-making."

In turn Stutzman models readiness to learn from respondent perspectives even as he dreams "of others . . . similarly motivated to help the free church build on its good tradition of biblical/communal discernment. . . ."

—*Michael A. King, Living Issues Discussion Series Editor*
(Full disclosure: King's primary work is as Dean, Eastern Mennonite Seminary, a division of Eastern Mennonite University. EMS is in the midst of ex-enhancing its role as a Discernment Training Center, including as host of a 2014 School for Leadership Training focused on discernment. Such activities may well benefit from resources connected to this book. King also maintains a limited role as Cascadia publisher. To minimize conflicts of interest, revenue traceable to sales connected with King's seminary activities will be paid to Eastern Mennonite University.)

·····················

Author's Preface

"May your kingdom come and your will be done, on earth as it is in heaven."

WITH THESE WORDS, Jesus taught his disciples to pray for God's will to be done in the world. One cannot rightly understand the ministry of Jesus without believing that God's will can and should be known among God's people. That is a core assumption of this book.

But how is God's will to be known in the world? *Discerning God's Will Together* assumes that God's will is made known primarily through a community of faith. When God's people are gathered in community, engaged with God's Word in Scripture, and enlightened by God's Spirit, they have the elements needed to discern God's will for our times.

Further, this book assumes that the same God who created the universe is on a mission to heal and redeem it—reconciling the entire creation to God's self. Jesus calls his followers to align themselves with God's mission—God's work—in the world. But how can we confidently know what God is doing to participate in this work? Again, prayerful discernment helps to show the way.

David Miller, a professor at Anabaptist Mennonite Biblical Seminary (AMBS), speaks of "tracking God" as one of the core tasks of the missional church. He employs the analogy of hunters, who often rely on clues to help them find wild game. A tuft of hair on a thorn bush, scratches on the side of a tree, a torn leaf—all point to the presence of animals passing through. So too, God leaves subtle but visible clues.

What then are the signs that God has been "passing through" an area, or that God has been at work?

In her research regarding the missional church, Lois Barrett, also of AMBS, discovered that many Christians find it difficult to speak of God as the subject of an active verb. She says this is true even when people are invited to respond to a direct question such as "What has God been doing in your life?" In response to that question, people are likely to name their own activities, presumably motivated by a desire to do God's will.

Discerning God's Will Together assumes that to really know God's will, we must learn to look for God in every aspect of life and then learn to align ourselves with the way we see God at work. This attentiveness lies at the heart of discernment of God's will, whether individual or corporate. There will always be a certain element of mystery to understanding God's will. Discernment will rarely be easy or totally clear to all participants. Nevertheless, this volume invites you to explore a discernment process with the confident assumption that God's people can learn both to identify and to align themselves with God's work in the world.

This book was first written as a thesis for Eastern Mennonite Seminary and is now being published with light revisions and updates as part of the EMS intent to serve the seminary community and the wider church as a center for training in discernment. As you read the book and ponder its scholarly insights, may God empower you both to know and to do God's will in the company of God's people.

—Ervin R. Stutzman
Executive Director, Mennonite Church USA
Harrisonburg, Virginia
January 2013

DISCERNING
GOD'S WILL
Together

CHAPTER 1
·······················

INTRODUCTION AND OVERVIEW

*E*VER SINCE PENTECOST, the church has debated the authority, interpretation, and use of Scripture. In modern biblical scholarship, the primary questions have focused on the accuracy of biblical reports and whether these ancient writings are relevant to contemporary life and culture. At the same time, the church wrestles with perplexing moral problems that defy simple solutions. Contemporary church communions are deeply divided in their approach to such issues as war and peace, divorce and remarriage among Christians, roles for men and women in family and church, and church membership or leadership roles for persons with same-sex preference or practice.

In its theological literature and official church documents, the church has declared that the Bible is to be interpreted within the church community through the Holy Spirit's guidance and illumination. Yet, as Inagrace Dietterich (1996) has asserted,

> detailed discussion of how this comes about and what it means for the faith and practice of the church is rare. While the scholars have exchanged papers and written books, knowledge of the message of the Bible and experience of its reality-shaping power have declined within the church. (1)

Further, although the Bible is acknowledged as the primary authority for faith and practice, differing modes of biblical interpretation lead to widely variant perspectives on difficult moral questions. This reality makes it difficult to move beyond polarization to corporate mission.

Therefore, I propose that *invoking the discernment function of free church ecclesiology can effectively aid the contemporary church in communal efforts at biblical interpretation, even amid conflict and controversy.*

Members of the free church can draw strength from a long tradition of communal discernment when facing difficult decisions. The church as a community of the Spirit is uniquely equipped to engage in group discernment. In recent years, as Marlin Miller asserts, the phrase "hermeneutical community" has been used "to suggest that the locus of scriptural interpretation is most properly the church, or that all members of the church should participate in the interpretation of Scripture, rather than limiting this task to specialists alone" (Kauffman and Koontz [K and K], 216). The gathered church brings corporate wisdom and strength to the task of interpreting Scripture for faithful Christian living.

Some scholarly works on biblical interpretation acknowledge the importance of balancing individual interpretation with that of the "hermeneutical community." A review of current theory in biblical interpretation reveals significant interest in the corporate dimension of the hermeneutical task. A few authors have explored the benefits and liabilities of such communal endeavors. Rarely, however, have these authors explicated at any length the means by which such communal interpretations best emerge. This study will attempt to bridge this practical and theoretical gap in the life of the free church.

More specifically, this study focuses on hermeneutic communities in the Anabaptist tradition. As proponents of the free church, the sixteenth-century Anabaptists worked at the task of biblical interpretation in ways that distinguished them both from other Reformers and the Roman Catholic Church. While contemporary Anabaptist historians differ in their assessment of Anabaptist practices, all agree that a study of their hermeneutics has relevance for today.[1] Anabaptist writings have contributed to modern understandings of group discernment processes as well as hermeneutical practices. The Anabaptists forged their hermeneutical approaches to Scripture during a time of intense controversy and rapid social change. The modern church can learn from them as it seeks to work through difficult issues in the current setting.

LIMITS OF THIS STUDY

To achieve clarity of focus, this study is deliberately limited in a number of ways. First of all, this study is limited to a discussion of free church ecclesiology as expressed in the Anabaptist tradition, beginning in the sixteenth century. While there are other authentic and applicable expressions of the free church, this paper focuses on the Anabaptist stream that now finds expression in the Mennonite churches of North America and their sister churches that relate to the Mennonite World Conference based in Strasburg, France.

Further, this book does not explore in depth the theological distinctions between free church hermeneutics and the interpretive approaches of other faith traditions. Neither does it explicate the theological assumptions that undergird Anabaptist hermeneutics or outline a particular hermeneutic process or approach to the biblical text.

Second, this study is limited to a review of secondary historical sources rather than primary documents, particularly in regard to sixteenth-century Anabaptists. While there are now many primary documents that have been translated into English, this study depends on the data gathering and analysis from a broad spectrum of documents by other scholars.

Third, this study is concerned with a relatively small segment in the spectrum of interpretative tasks. At the far left is the task of the historical-critical scholar and the linguist, finding the meaning of the Scripture for the original hearers and translating it to create analogical meaning in our contemporary world. At the far right is the task of the pastor and the congregation, applying the imperatives of Scripture in a particular time and place. The further right on the spectrum, the more that interpretation involves discernment on moral and practical issues. While there are communal processes that may be invoked in the historical-critical task of exegesis,[2] this study is concerned primarily with the communal discernment processes based on the exegetical work already done by others. It does include, however, communal exegesis of the cultural and moral situation in which the worshiping community is located.

Fourth, the vision set forth in this study is limited primarily to biblical interpretation in a congregational setting. As noted above, much contemporary biblical interpretation is erudite, restricted primarily to communities of scholars. While scholarly studies provide the foundation for much of the material used in congregational Bible study, the more critical insights of scholars often remain out of reach of the ordinary person in the pew.[3] This study assumes that communal discernment in most congregations depends largely on a straightforward reading of the biblical text rather than studies of original biblical languages, complex exegesis, or sophisticated analysis. While scholars contribute an essential piece to the exegetical process, the average layperson in a discernment process will not draw deeply on those insights in a typical discernment process.

UNDERLYING ASSUMPTIONS

This study assumes an orthodox view of Scripture, theology, ecclesiology, and Christology, particularly as expressed in the *Confession of Faith in a Mennonite Perspective*. While this paper includes discussion of viewpoints which differ from or challenge this confessional statement, it is not designed to undermine an historic orthodox position. In the same vein, this study builds on the insights of doctrinal or positional statements adopted by the Mennonite Church over the years, including its statements on biblical interpretation. (See Stutzman, 2011, for in-depth exploration of such statements.)

Second, in the discussion regarding communal discernment, this study assumes the presence of healthy congregations or groups with openness and ability to flex. Further, the discussion regarding conflict management assumes relatively low levels of disagreement or conflict, where group members are committed to one another and are able to focus on substantive issues for discernment. Where congregants are committed to win-lose propositions or are committed to punishing or ridding themselves of those who disagree with them, the conflict management techniques explained here will not likely be effective.

Third, this study assumes the freedom of church groups to creatively discern God's truth through application of Scripture in the contemporary setting, rather than simply relying on traditional interpretations of a biblical text. I recognize that my church leadership roles have clearly shaped this assumption.

Prior to my current role as the executive director of Mennonite Church USA, I served the church in the roles of pastor, overseer, mission administrator, denominational moderator, and seminary dean. I have come to think of the church as a community of communities, each with its own history, values, and group identity. In many of the church gatherings that represent various communities, we struggle to find unity amid disparate individual interpretations or applications of Scripture. I have valued the times when, through communal discernment, we have found creative ways to apply scriptural understandings in current church situations.

I resided for a time in Lancaster County, Pennsylvania, where the concentration of Mennonites is the highest in North America. Mennonites have divided into many different groups; Lancaster County probably reflects a fuller spectrum of belief and practice than any other place. Particularly during the merger process that formed Mennonite Church USA, I witnessed the separation of groups that did not want to join the new denomination, citing differences on the basis of issues of biblical interpretation and application as part of their rationale.

I now reside in Harrisonburg, Virginia, as part of a Mennonite community linked to Eastern Mennonite University, where I once served as a professor and academic dean. The conflicts that sometimes result from the tensions of "town and gown" may at times illustrate differing approaches to biblical interpretation and application. Most notably, the university reaches out to different religious faith communities through its Center for Justice and Peacebuilding, at times exploring religious texts from outside the Christian faith.

Further, I have worked as a mediator in church conflict, particularly as a function of my leadership role as moderator. I have often been called to help when a church felt the need for outside assistance. Thus, my view of conflict, polarity management, and discernment has been shaped by my leadership experiences in actual discernment processes or church conflicts. This may help to explain the disproportionate space given to conflict resolution and polarity management in this volume.

ORGANIZATION OF THE STUDY

This study is organized into six chapters. This initial chapter introduces the research problem, sets forth a thesis for discussion, reveals underlying assumptions, and explains the overall organization of the study.

Chapters Two and Three examine the contributions which Anabaptist scholars have made to the discussions on ecclesiology, discernment, and biblical interpretation. Both chapters provide a review of relevant literature. Chapter Two focuses particularly on the relevance of ecclesiology as the basis for understanding the role of the church as a discerning community. A proper understanding of the *nature* of the church is foundational to an understanding of the *functions* of the church. Chapter Three focuses particularly the matter of biblical interpretation, both in its historical and contemporary expressions in theory and practice.

Chapter Four introduces a focused discussion on some of the difficulties and differences that church communities face in their attempts at discernment. Certainly, not all discernment processes involve overt tension and conflict. But since discernment requires judgment, most discernment processes involve some clash of interests and values which must be addressed. Particularly amid controversy engendered by social change, the church experiences tension and uncertainty. Many times, these tensions will never be fully resolved, since they arise from values that are indispensable to Christian living, yet lie at opposing poles.

Any process of corporate discernment must take these polarities seriously, since many of them are deeply imbedded in Scripture itself. A proper understanding of paradoxical biblical truths will contribute to healthy corporate processes of biblical interpretation in communities of faith. Similarly, the creative use of principles for conflict management can enable the church to work through times of difficulty. This chapter, therefore, seeks to provide perspective and guidance for working through difficulties that arise amid controversy and change.

Chapter Five sets forth a vision for cultivating the development of discerning hermeneutic communities in the contemporary congregational setting. Again, to cite Dietterich (1996), "the cultivation of communities of faithful and wise hearers, readers, and doers of the Bible is central to the authentic discernment of vision and direction, the development of energy and motivation, and the stimulation of broad and active participation" (1). Therefore, this chapter examines the task of discernment as it may be expressed in three basic areas of church life-worship, community, and mission. Lastly, this chapter explicates several examples of contemporary networks other than the congregation that serve as hermeneutic communities to enable the church to faithfully apply the Scriptures in the vortex of contemporary life.

Chapter Six concludes the work of this book. It provides a brief summary of the arguments in this study and makes recommendations for further study of ideas that meet at the intersection of ecclesiology, hermeneutics, and communal discernment.

NOTES

1. Swartley (1995, 65f.), for example, explores the following two theses, and expresses the opinion that they are both true, yet in different ways:

"From the Anabaptists we learn little of value for the contemporary use and interpretation of Scripture."

"From the Anabaptists we learn almost all we need to know about the contemporary use and interpretation of Scripture."

2. For example, the writers of the Believers Commentary Series (Herald Press) work alongside mentors and other scholars as they go about their work.

3. See for example Walter Wink (1989, 17) or James Smart (1970, 16f.).

CHAPTER 2
••••••••••••••••••••••••

THE FREE CHURCH AS A COMMUNITY FOR DISCERNMENT

THE CONCEPT OF A FREE CHURCH

The free church tradition stands in stark contrast to Constantinianism, where the church is established and supported by the state. The free church implies a church relatively free from political entanglements or obligation. The early church was largely free from political alliances until the age of Constantine in the fourth century. While some in the church were grateful for Constantine's interest in and protection of the church, others were highly opposed. Thus, Ross Bender traces the beginning of the free church to the followers of Donatus in the fourth century who challenged the church system with these words: "What does the emperor have to do with the church?" He also named others who followed in their train: "the Cathari of the eleventh century, the Waldenses of the twelfth, the Lollards of fourteenth-century England, and the Hussites of Bohemia" (19).

The early church, which began on the social margins of society, became established in Rome, the power center of the world at that time. Under Constantinian Christendom, the mission of the church was largely perpetuated by centers of power and prestige. In John Driver's words, this was "a sociological and missiological reversal of the Christian apostolate of the first century" (1997, 226). Consequently, after centuries of Christendom, the images of transformation in the New Testament have largely lost their symbolic power because "the church has ceased to be a witnessing (martyr) community, dependent on the Spirit of God alone" (227).

One might analyze many facets of Constantinianism, not all germane. For purposes of this book, it is essential to recognize that the ecclesiology of Christendom and that of the free church are radically different. Yoder (1994) asserts that

> The most pertinent fact about the new state of things after Constantine and Augustine is not that Christians were no longer persecuted and began to be privileged, nor that emperors built churches and presided over ecumenical deliberations about the Trinity; what matters is that the two visible realities, church and world, were fused. There is no longer anything to call "world"; state economy, art, rhetoric, superstition, and war have all been baptized. (57)

Yoder continues:

> The attempt to reverse the New Testament relationship of church and world, making faith invisible and the Christianization of the world a historic achievement with the institutional forms, was undertaken in good faith but has backfired, having had the sole effect of raising the autonomy of unbelief to a higher power. (61).

Again Yoder asserts,

> The fundamental wrongness of the vision of Christendom is its illegitimate takeover of the world; its ascription of a Christian loyalty or duty to those who have made no confession and, thereby, its denying to the non-confessing creation the freedom of unbelief that the nonresistance of God in creation gave to a rebellious humanity. (109)

Christendom as a system introduces a blurring of boundaries between world and church, between state politics and church government, between belief and unbelief. Therefore, the nature and identity of the church as depicted in the New

Testament are severely compromised. The New Testament vision of a people "set apart for God" (cf. 1 Pet. 2:9) is distorted. The free church is a missional society, a community of believers committed to knowing and doing the will of God not matter what the political cost. In contrast to Christendom, the free church is a contrast society, often standing at odds with the values and overt expressions of the dominant culture.

Bender expresses the essence of the free church in simple language. It is "free to do the will of God—free not only from political commitments but free to follow the Holy Spirit in whatever patterns of church organization . . . that he leads us to" (6). Bender suggests that several other terms, each with its own limitations, express part of the free church essence. One might use labels such as the "faithful," "believers," "disciples," or "Anabaptists" (6). The first three of these suggest loyalty to Jesus Christ as Lord, as opposed to governing authorities.

Bender asserts that a distinctive pattern of church order grew out of the free church nature and identity. Three of the characteristics he identifies are highly germane to this discussion as it relates to discernment and biblical interpretation:

> The first principle of church order was that the church is constituted on the basis of voluntary covenants among persons who confess their faith freely in Jesus Christ. Two important distinctive marks of the true church are discipline and dialogue.
>
> There was an emphasis on the priesthood of all believers. They also provided for a significant role for women in the church.
>
> Decision-making was based upon consensus. There was a "talking up" of the issues until the brethren were agreed and could say "it seemed good to the Holy Spirit and to us." There was a strong emphasis upon the doctrine of the Holy Spirit. (86)

The concept of Christendom did not end with the sixteenth-century Reformation. The expressions of Christendom simply took on a different look and feel. In Stuart Murray's words,

> The Reformers set up alternative expressions of Christendom which fragmented the monolithic empire but kept many of the Constantinian assumptions and framework.

> While they insisted on the freedom of the church for bibli-
> cal interpretation, they in fact often bowed to secular au-
> thorities. (1992, 330-1)

Murray identified this system of biblical interpretation as a reflection of the "hermeneutics of order." Anabaptists, the progenitors of the free church, insisted on the right of the church to interpret Scripture apart from political authority, labeled by some as "hermeneutics of obedience" (McGrath) or "hermeneutics of discipleship."

Yoder (1994) suggests that we might describe the current situation of church and state as a form of "neo-Constantinianism." He believes that since 1648, when the wars of religion in Europe ended, the fusion between church and state has tightened, "since the wars of religion linked particular churches with particular national governments in a way that had not obtained in the Middle Ages. Now the church is servant, not of humanity at large but of a particular society; not of the entire society but of a particular dominating class" (195).

Consequently, some people of other faith traditions can only think of Christian faith in the light of the Crusades or the Holocaust. With increasing balkanization and the growing familiarity of war between Muslims and Christians, we must, as Yoder asserts, "disentangle Jesus from the Christ of Byzantium or Torquemada." "The disavowal of Constantine is then not a distraction but the condition of the historical seriousness of the confession that it is Jesus Christ who is Lord" (Yoder, 261). Blaming the blindness of a previous generation for having been identified with unworthy political causes overlooks the fundamental error of having identified with a particular power structure in the first place (Yoder 200).

When the church is dominant in society, it significantly affects the presuppositions with which it approaches Scripture (cf. Murray 1992, 329). Scripture tends to be interpreted in ways that maintain the existing order which benefits both church and state. From a free church perspective, the assumptions of Christendom distort biblical interpretation. Murray asserts: "A significant contribution of Anabaptism, then, is its development of a hermeneutics that is largely devoid of Constantinian assumptions and conclusions in biblical interpretation" (1992, 342).

Although not all are Anabaptist in orientation, several of the recent studies (Barton, 2012; Fendall et. al., 2007; and Glick, 2004) regarding the practice of congregational discernment focus on the nature of the free church as a place where God can speak to the gathered assembly. These studies assume that gathered groups, such as congregations, must not ignore the long history of doctrines and biblical hermeneutics of the broader church, yet they are free to seek God's will in the application of the scripture to their specific context.

THE COMMUNAL NATURE OF THE FREE CHURCH

Jesus gave his disciples authority for ministry, symbolized by "the keys of the kingdom of heaven" (Matt. 16:19). Further, Jesus gave authority to the church for "binding" and "loosing" when they gather in his name (Matt. 18:18-20). Kraus (63) interprets the passage in several statements that follow: "The disciple community has been authorized to make binding decisions in the name and spirit of Christ."

> The church's authority does not reside in its status as a superior religious institution superceding Israel. It has authority only because Jesus continues to be with it. That authority resides in the church's *dependence on Christ* and its *authenticity as a disciple community*. Therefore there must be discernment and agreement that its decisions represent the true spirit and will of Jesus.

Individuals alone cannot fully comprehend or represent the will of God. Binding and loosing happen as actions of a moral community in the gathered church.[1]

Weaver (120) asserts that

> the church which follows Jesus is a new social reality—a community. That is, to follow Jesus involves a new way of life which expresses itself in redeemed attitudes and relationships among people both within and without the church. This communal or social orientation does not deny individuality or the personal nature of one's faith, but says, rather, that the individual's faith attains its meaning in terms of the *believing community*.

Kraus (28) agrees:

Modern insights from anthropology, sociology, and psychology confirm the biblical presupposition that the basic
human unit is not the independent individual before God
but the *individual in community* before God. We become
self-conscious individuals only in community relationships. Indeed, we might say that personhood is the gift of
the familial community.

The increasing privatization of faith and assertion of individual autonomy stand at odds with the biblical vision. True
disciples do not walk alone.

Kraus (199) describes the biblical vision with a metaphori-
cal reference to the city. He asserts that "city" (Gk. *polis*), understood in its connotation in the ancient world, could be used
as a synonym for the idea of community in our world today.
The city provided security, abundance, and civil order. Abra-
ham rejected Ur of the Chaldees for a city whose builder and
maker was God. The book of Revelation pictures a city, where
Christ himself is the light. In Kraus' mind, this is a highly symbolic description of the "consummated community of salvation" (199n1). Harold S. Bender (1962) describes the church as
a "holy community which has fellowship with Christ and
whose members have fellowship with each other" (42).

The community of believers is a community of the Spirit, a
concrete expression of God's ongoing work in the world. "It is
characterized by the "fruit of the Spirit"—the "more excellent
way" of love. It is not created by sacramental consecration, theological announcement, ecstatic experience, or moralistic
achievement. If such a reality of the Spirit does not exist, the
gospel has little meaning in our contemporary secular existence" (Kraus, 30).

The community of the Spirit is an apostolic fellowship, "an
assembly of persons who share a common Spirit, Lord, conviction, and mission. A common loyalty is signified in baptism
and a shared life" (Kraus, 125). The Holy Spirit of God is the
"glue" that holds the community of disciples together. As
vividly portrayed in the book of Acts, the Spirit empowers the
community of believers, causes it to grow, and grants the powers of discernment (2:17; 4:31, 5:3-4; 8:15-17; 11:15-18; 15: 28). It
is this same Spirit which calls and sends forth people into God's
mission (Acts 13:1-3).

The free church is not only communal, it is a missional society . While the Holy Spirit calls and the church commissions persons for apostolic itinerant ministry (Acts 13:1-3), the community is also, by its very nature, a corporate witness to God's grace. The empowering and transforming work of the Holy Spirit amid the disciple community calls people to faith (1 Cor. 14:25; 1 Thess. 1:4-10; 1 Pet. 2:9). The Holy Spirit grants gifts to each member not only for the mutual building up of the community but also for ministry to the world (Rom. 12:3-8, 1 Cor. 12:4-31; Eph. 4:11-13).

As some have suggested, "covenant community" is not a biblical phrase per se, but it faithfully communicates the essence of other rich communal metaphors such as the "body of Christ," the "people of God," or "the priesthood of all believers"). This latter designation was given its most definite and radical meaning by the early Anabaptists, who used the term to imply a lay apostolate. Every member was to be a missionary.

Some advocates of the free church have interpreted the vision of an apostolic community to preclude the need for strong or effective pastoral leadership.[2] Further, an egalitarian vision for ministry may be understood as a mandate for egalitarian and/or democratic means of decision making. This idea, then, brings us to a discussion of the discerning function of the free church community.

THE DISCERNING FUNCTION OF THE FREE CHURCH COMMUNITY

Franklin Littell (77), a scholar of historical Anabaptism, believes that the "apostolate of the laity," as a free church concept, empowers ordinary church members to make decisions as they are led by the Holy Spirit. Further, he believes that "the purpose of discussion in the church, whether in the widest and most catholic setting of international seminars and magazines or in the intimacy of face-to-face groups in a single congregation, is the same: to discover God's will for His whole people, to plan how best to express that Will in concrete witness." Just as individuals need to exercise discernment that issues in particular decisions, so do groups. Particularly in the context of the church, group discernment is needed to discover God's will in keeping with God's purposes for God's people.

John Howard Yoder (1994) eschews situation ethics, but believes that both principle and context may be fruitfully considered through Spirit-led communal discernment. The "two dimensions can meet with integrity" through the work of the Holy Spirit; "not a reasoning process but a mode of God's own working. That this is what the Holy Spirit does is stated in John 14-16, illustrated anecdotally throughout the book of Acts, and projected procedurally in 1 Corinthians 14" (122). God speaks in the group context.

Redekop (127) suggests that "dependence upon the working of the Holy Spirit is imperative, and the absolute starting point. Without the power of the Holy Spirit, everything is of no avail." In his mind, only the working of the Holy Spirit can enable the free church to overcome the negative and distorting effects of total ideology on group discernment.

Discernment, then, is one of the functions of the free church community when it is gathered in Christ's name. It reflects the moral nature of the church. "A view of the church as a community of corporate discernment and action under the leading of the Holy Spirit was historically among the most distinctive understandings of Anabaptist-Mennonites" (*Pastor-Growing*, 33). In the context of corporate worship, community, and mission, discernment is an expression of the presence of God's Spirit in the community of faith.

To sharpen the focus of this discussion on discernment, it is appropriate to consider more precisely the mandate for and meaning of discernment, as well as some barriers that prevent adequate discernment in the community of believers.

The Mandate for Discernment

The communal mandate for discernment is rooted in the saying of Jesus in Matthew 18:15-20. Sometimes called the "rule of Christ," the latter passage places responsibility for binding and loosing on the community gathered in Christ's name. Driver (42) suggests that the church was "understood basically as the community in which binding and loosing occur." "Where this process does not take place the church has not been realized according to the fullest intention of Jesus."

To bind meant to withhold pardon, to retain (sins) and, therefore, to exclude from the fellowship of the community. To loose meant to absolve, to pardon, to forgive (sins). This meaning becomes clear when one compares the parallel passages in Luke 17:3 and John 20:23. The general context of Matthew 18 which deals with forgiveness supports this interpretation. (Driver, 44)

However, Driver elaborates,

binding and loosing also carried another meaning. To bind meant to forbid, or to make obligatory, or to order a certain course of moral behavior. To loose meant to permit, or to leave a person free to make an ethical choice among various alternatives. This was the way in which these terms were used by the Jewish rabbis of Jesus' time. (44)

For Driver (45), forgiveness and reconciliation are closely linked to moral discernment in two ways:

(1) The process of restoring brothers and sisters through repentance and forgiveness presupposes a common moral basis. The ethical norms by which sin is recognized are known and shared mutually, thus providing criteria for evaluating offense. (2) The process of conversation aimed at restoration is the best way to clarify, to test, and then either to confirm or to change community ethics. This process leads to a new experience in discernment of God's will and is the path to restoration and reconciliation among brothers and sisters.

Yoder (1984, 27) claims that the "rule of Christ" as a concept of binding and loosing traces its roots back to some common source in Reformation history, having been used by Martin Bucer, the radical Zwinglians, and Martin Luther in 1526. This concept is similar to what modern social ethicists label as "practical moral reasoning," whereby "A transcendent moral ratification is claimed for the decisions made in the conversation of two or three or more, in a context of forgiveness and in the juridical form of listening to several witnesses." Whereas governing authorities of the state can only pass judgment based on civil law, the church appeals to a higher moral authority. While church members obey civil laws that do not offend conscience, the church governs its communal life by a different set of rules, based on biblical ethics.

Communal discernment enables the church to stand as a contrast society. It provides protection for the believers in a individualistic world. In Yoder's (1984, 40) words, "We need a communal instrument of moral reasoning in the light of faith precisely to defend the decision-maker against the stream of conformity to his own world's self-evidence. Practical moral reasoning, if Christian, must always be expected to be at some point subversive." He reasons: "If moral discernment is not culture-critical, it has lost its connection with the gospel of grace and has fallen into the ratification of things as they are and choices as I want them" (Yoder 1984, 43).

Burkholder (1965, 131) argues that communal discernment processes have always been a part of Anabaptist-Mennonite history. Congregations asked baptismal candidates if they were ready to give and receive counsel. "That means that one opened oneself up to God's direction so that one might be a contributing factor to the understanding of the congregation." In the same vein, Yoder (1994, 338) argues that Anabaptists refused to baptize their babies, not because infants could not have an experience of faith, but because "one who requests baptism submits to the mutual obligation of giving and receiving counsel in the congregation; this is what a child cannot do." "Far from being the extreme expression of individualism, the baptism of believers is thus the foundation of the most sweeping communal responsibility of all members for the life of all members" (340). Burkholder (131) conveys similar convictions: "It must be said that a congregation comes to order when it addresses itself under the inspiration of the Holy Spirit and with reference to the Bible to a great question. That is church in the very best sense of the word."

The Meaning of Discernment

Discernment is a biblical concept (cf. Rom. 12:2, 1 Cor. 6:1-9; 12:8-10, Heb. 5:14, and Phil. 1:10). As defined in this study, discernment is a means by which people of faith come to understand God's will for a particular situation. Especially in the Old Testament, *certain individuals* were reputed to be wise and discerning. But by the very nature of the church in the New

Testament, the people of God are called to be discerning *as a group*.[3] Sometimes, the most discerning people in a congregation are those who are little noticed.

Discernment is a process by which believers anticipate God's presence, look for God's guidance, and listen for God's call. Discernment "involves the interplay of critical reflection with the kind of purposive action which issues from the response of obedience to the will of God" (R. Bender, 167). The words "to judge," "to watch," and "to be alert" carry similar meanings in Scripture.

Burkholder (116) contends that the hardest question a church can ask itself is how it can know the will of God in relationship to the world of today. In his mind, "discernment is the clue to New Testament ethics." "They would look at an event in history and they would ask themselves as a community under the Holy Spirit, 'What is the meaning of this? Is it good or bad? Is it for Christ or against Christ?'" In contemporary language, one might call this "exegesis of the situation."

Discernment is a key activity of a believing church. Lederach (1980, 117) asserts: "Christians are to discern because they are living under God who is also discerning. God's discernment and Christian discernment are to coincide. Christians are to live so that they are approved now and also in the judgment." Burkholder (1963, 1072) stresses that "the challenge before the peace churches is to become discerning congregations which 'test' whether the authenticating reality of the obedient life is present today, i.e., whether there is a word from the Lord."

Redekop (1970, 133) describes discernment as three primary activities:

1) It engages in deep and intense study of what the Scriptures and the Spirit of Christ command and demand its followers to do. 2) It analyzes the sources and meaning of God's Word in terms of its original meanings and what they are saying today. 3) It is concerned about defining the nature of Christian life and obedience in contemporary terms.

George Schemel offers the following definition: "an experiential knowledge of self in the congruence of the object of choice with one's fundamental religious orientation." This implies the essential need to know oneself, to know the issue, and to know God. Schemel views discernment as the means by which we look for God's direction, and God's Word to us.[4]

Schemel's definition, particularly as it relates to self-knowledge, seems to imply individual discernment. Yet the community of faith, to function effectively as a discerning community, must understand its own identity and calling[5] to make wise, discerning decisions. Without an adequate understanding of its nature and mission, a church cannot function effectively as a discerning community.

Barriers to Discernment

There are many barriers to communal discernment, far too numerous to elucidate here in depth. But a few demand at least brief attention, for the sake of clarifying the essential components of discernment, which follow in the next section.

One of the primary barriers to communal discernment in our contemporary world is individualism, which militates against communal practice. As Bellah et. al. have shown, a strong sense of individualism dominates the U.S. social and religious scene. Rejection of authority commonly accompanies individualism, so that both civil and ecclesial authorities have less influence in people's lives. When individualism runs rampant, the corporate authority and mission of the church are seriously undermined, as is the ability of the church to practice corporate discernment.

A second barrier to discernment is a textualism that separates the Bible from the work of the Spirit in community. As explained by Dietterich (1996, 1), there can be a tendency to separate the Spirit from the Word by viewing the Bible as a collection of inerrant truth or facts about God, the world, humanity, and salvation which are self-explanatory. It privileges individual interpretations of the Bible apart from the "worship, counsel, and testing of the Spirit-gathered church."

Watson (102) discusses "textualism" in a similar vein, calling it orthodoxy without the Holy Spirit." Again, "literalism" is a label which conveys the tendency to elevate the words of Scripture without enjoying the liberating power of the Spirit which brings life. Similarly, a bare intellectualism may view the Bible primarily as a set of propositions, abstract statements, and words. Corporate discernment values not only words and concepts, but actions and relationships.

A third barrier—spiritualism—stands at the opposite spectrum from textualism. Spiritualism separates the Spirit from the Word. Individuals experience this barrier when they rely on their own "spirit, heart, reason, intuition, or experience," and consider as irrelevant such church activities as "baptism, eucharist, preaching, forgiveness, and Bible study" (Dietterich, 1996, 2). Experience is unduly elevated over comprehension of the written word as understood by the community of faith. Spiritualism may also take the form of anti-intellectualism, which rejects the serious exegetical study of Scripture which is necessary for faithful corporate discernment.

Particularly in the West, affluence often serves as a fourth barrier to corporate discernment. As Swartley (1982, 248) and Watson (101) have observed, wealth and materialism bombard individuals with a false seduction that steal away commitment to Christ and the church. It is often during times of economic stress or persecution that the church is most conscious of its unique calling. When the church is wealthy, its ability to discern the hard sayings of Jesus is compromised. Affluence dulls the mind and perception to spiritual things, rendering genuine discernment on some matters difficult if not impossible.

Finally, humanism poses a serious barrier to corporate discernment. Secular humanism particularly stands in opposition to the claim of the Spirit-filled community that they are hearing the voice of God in their midst. Humanism asserts the primacy of human thought, sometimes rejecting scriptural authority. Modern biblical scholarship has adopted the tenets of humanism on many fronts, suppressing the claims of divine authority and power. This form of liberalism tends to make human reason the judge of truth. Without a strong commitment to God's word, the ability of the church to effectively discern God's truth is severely compromised.

COMPONENTS OF COMMUNAL DISCERNMENT

With what matters is communal discernment concerned? Where does it take place? Who participates? How do they go about it? These questions are addressed below.

The Matter for Discernment

Burkholder (1965, 132) suggests that ethical decisions are the most important decisions a congregation can make. In his mind, "controversial questions are often the important questions, and controversial questions should be brought before the church. And if the church can't handle controversial questions, then it is under the domination of the principalities and the powers."

While ethical or moral questions could indeed be the most important questions faced by the church, there are many other matters that may profitably be brought before the body for corporate discernment. For example, many churches use some form of communal discernment to choose from among a number of candidates for pastoral leadership. Others use communal discernment to decide among options for church facilities. Still others employ communal discernment to help determine the church's missional direction. This book, however, will attempt to demonstrate that the church may profitably use communal discernment in determining the proper interpretation and application of the Scriptures in the life of the church.

George Schemel and Judith Roemer believe that discernment works best when the matter for discernment is clearly presented in a concise declarative statement which represents a change from the status quo. The community can then discuss the cons and pros of the statement, discerning what God is saying amid the community.

The Context for Discernment

As stated above, the congregation is the primary context for discernment. While discernment may take place in the weekly time of worship, other contexts within the congregation are just as common—Christian Education classes, membership meetings, or cell groups.

Again, communal discernment may take place in a variety of contexts besides the congregation, ranging in scope from the primary social group to virtual communities scattered around the globe. The nature of the discernment will vary considerably depending on the particular context.

Redekop argues that group structures influence the cognitive and behavior processes of individuals, so that koinonia groups and small congregations function more effectively than large congregations to help people to submit to the Spirit of God. He asserts that to be really effective, people need relationships along three dimensions: 1) length of duration in time, 2) depth of intimacy, and 3) breadth of knowledge of each other's roles and positions. In essence, these are a description of primary social relationships. "It is only in the primary relationship that the Christian gospel can become effective" (Redekop, 131).

Therefore, he believes that to launch groups that work to help Christians live like Christians, the church must enable the formation of small groups. This must be done by 1) recognizing "the theological and ecclesiastical significance of peer (koinonia) groups, 2) helping to form groups under the guidance of the Holy Spirit, and 3) making sure that peer groups possess "sufficient biblical and theological understanding so that they can develop peer group standards which are consistent with the biblical tradition" (Redekop, 143). He asserts further that groups larger than twenty-five can be helpful in worship, teaching, and serving, but not in primary relationships. These settings become primarily an interaction between a group and its leader, not an interaction between members of the group with each other.

Schemel and Roemer often work with larger groups of people, yet taking into account the need for primary relationships. In their model of communal discernment, they employ the use of small groups as part of the process. Participants work with the same group of eight-ten persons throughout the process, with members of each small group reporting to the larger group via a reporter. The communal discernment process thus incorporates time for individual prayer and reflection, small group discussion, as well as large group worship, prayer, and reporting. In a similar way, most congregations can provide several contexts for communal discernment, depending on the matter at hand.

Level of Agreement Sought

While it is rare for all participants in a discernment process to agree on every detail, consensus is the goal for most free church communities. An apostolic pattern of decision-making is described in the text from Acts 15:28, "It seemed good to the Holy Spirit and to us." Littell comments on this passage: "This is not simple democracy, but rather a way of hearing God" (Littell, 81). In Littell's mind, the most perfect democracy exists where the "sense of the meeting" is clearly known without a vote. The Quakers, well-known for free church patterns of decision making, generally postpone decisions until consensus emerges from the group.

Consensus does not imply total agreement, however. It may also be considered consensus if everyone agrees that the group decision is the best way forward, even though it may not represent their own opinion. Some may consider it consensus if persons who disagree with the decision agree not to oppose or block the group's decision, especially after they have had opportunity to thoroughly air a contrary point of view and have a sense of being respected and understood.

Participants in Discernment

As noted above, the concept of the "priesthood of all believers" may be used as a basis for enlisting all members of the church in communal discernment. For Littell (70), this concept implies that every church member has "not the right but the obligation to bring his insights and his concerns to the common table. The understanding tends properly not to the debasement of the priesthood but to the elevation of the laity." Speaking of discernment regarding church discipline, Littell (89-90) opines:

> If decision on basic matters, whether the matter at hand involves theological, ethical, moral or organizational discipline, is to be reached by a small ruling group, by professional theologians and canon lawyers, or perhaps by powers outside the Christian Church entirely, then there is no foundation for discussion. If, however, the whole Church is to be enlisted, then the process of reaching and sustaining the discipline is also the process of enlisting the whole *laos theou* in the developing of the consensus.

Driver (38) argues in a similar vein:

> Church structures which make it difficult for individuals to share fully in responsibility for the life of the Christian

community deny the true nature of the body of Christ. Structures which relegate responsibility into the hands of a few, no matter if they are congregational or inter-congregational, only encourage passive participation and loss of interest in brotherhood welfare by the members.

There seems to be a scholarly consensus that in the free church every member participates to some extent in matters of communal discernment. Yet members function in particular and diverse ways, as noted below.

Interaction between Participants

Smucker believes that the mandate for communal discernment comes from the sayings of Jesus on binding and loosing, discussed above. Therefore, he conceives of the interactive process of discernment as both human and divine. It is human in that God works through the human instrumentality of the body of Christ. It is transcendent in that the Spirit leads people toward a common sense of direction (Acts 15:28) and to new horizons of vision and hope. He concludes:

> The challenge in spiritual discernment is to embrace both the human and the transcendent at the same time. God's way becomes known through human interaction: in prayer and worship, dialogue and deliberation, disagreement and resolution, decision and action. Disagreement and conflict in the body of Christ is meant to bring us to humility and mutual submission. (Smucker, 3)

Perhaps it is true, as Redekop (137) contends, that most church groups, whether hierarchical or "democratic," are not structured for in-depth discernment. Doctors of law, priests, and theologians have attempted to determine God's will without intimate interaction with fellow believers who are expected to accept that interpretation. Particularly when the group is dealing with controversial issues, God's will cannot really be discerned without depth of trust in the interaction, removal of masks and superficialities, and the emergence of fundamental motivation on individual lives.

Persons too often come to discernment processes with hidden agenda. They tend to "put their best foot forward." As Redekop (136) has argued: "Discernment (theologizing) can take place only as entire persons relate to others in their entirety, so that the gospel is actually incarnated in the breadth and complexity of the reality of the human conditions and needs and the search for answers to these needs." Further, Redekop (157) contends, "In the discernment process, confrontation is crucial since it helps prevent personal, subjective, idiosyncratic, bizarre, deceptive, and all other 'unsanctified' motives from taking precedence over the objective import of the gospel intent." "Were all theologians to test their theologizing with a small primary group of fellow Christians, much irresponsible thinking would be avoided."

At times, genuine discernment will of necessity involve conversation between those who hold opposite viewpoints on crucial issues. Such conversation generally works best when construed as dialogue. While some eschew dialogue as inherently liberalizing, there is precedent for genuine dialogue in the Scriptures. Kraus argues (185) that Jesus entered into a dialogical relationship with humankind by coming to earth as a man. Paul was dialogical in spirit when he declared himself as a debtor both to the Greeks and barbarians, both to the wise and the foolish" (Rom. 1:14). Kraus opines that "dialogue does not rule out conviction, explanation, or even persuasion. To be taken seriously in a dialogue one must have a clear self-identity and intelligent convictions. Mutual explanation and questioning is the essential form of dialogue" (186-7).

Kraus argues that "proper humility and respect for the partner in conversation is imperative in dialogue" (187). He contrasts unilateral conversation with dialogue:

> The monological stance is argumentative. The debater aims to prove a point and "win" the debate. The dialogical stance is informative and confessional. The witness aims to win the confidence of the partner through a sincere, honest relationship.

Dialogue will not always result in consensus, however. It may rather result in greater differentiation and a hardening of positions. In fact, serious dialogue may lead to the mutual conclusion that the opposing parties can no longer work together.

Yoder (1984, 29f.) draws from a number of Scriptures in an attempt to outline what the shape of the conversation might be in the process of communal moral discernment. More specifically, he identifies various functions performed by different "agents" in the interaction among participants. For him, 1 Corinthians 14:29 shows that there will be Agents of Direction. That is, some prophetic voices will show direction. Their contribution will be weighed by others. Matthew 13:52 shows that "the community will be aided by Agents of Memory." These are scribes who search through the treasures of the communal storehouse for relevant memories. "The scribe as practical moral reasoner does not judge or decide anything, but he (or she) remembers expertly, charismatically the store of memorable, identity-confirming acts of faithfulness praised and of failure repented." James 3:18 and other Scriptures show that "the community will be guided by Agents of Linguistic Self-Consciousness." Yoder asserts that the references to the tongue in James likely have more to do with the power of language than with gossip or impulsive utterance. He concludes that there should not be many teachers (persons who shape communal direction by the skilled use of language) "because not many of those who use language are aware of its temptations."

In Yoder's mind (33), the Scriptures having to do with "bishops," overseers," and supervisors show that "the community will be guided by Agents of Order and Due Process." "The moderator or facilitator as practical moral reasoner is accountable for assuring that everyone else is heard, and that the conclusions reached are genuinely consensual." "The apostolic prototype is the Lord's brother James, summing up (Acts 15:13) the mutually acceptable conclusion of a meeting in which minds had been changed because people had listened to one another." Finally, Yoder concludes, "it belongs to the elder/moderator/bishop/shepherd to ask whether and how each proposed polarity or complementarity will 'edify' (i.e., construct a place to be at home together)" (37).

While Yoder's listing of process agents is helpful, it is certainly not exhaustive. He does not mention, for example, agents gifted for discernment of spirits (1 Cor. 12:10) or agents devoted to intercession and/or prayer for discernment (Phil. 1:9-11). Communal discernment draws both strength and insight from God, who works in ways beyond human ability.

Nevertheless, there are some timely procedures in discernment processes that will prove helpful in a range of contexts. What follows below, then, is a brief exposition of several different procedures, in terms of steps or stages, that may be used in communal discernment processes.

Steps or Stages in the Discernment Process

Scholars and practitioners from different traditions have suggested processes by which discernment can be exercised and decisions made in congregational settings.[6] This study will briefly summarize several such studies as examples to consider.

Smucker outlines a number of steps for moral discernment in congregational meetings: 1) assessing the situation, 2) clarifying responsibility, 3) developing a plan, 4) preparing the congregation, and 5) facilitating the process. These steps are designed to help a congregation make decisions regarding moral issues. In similar manner as other practitioners, Smucker asserts that it is important to develop and follow a plan for the discernment process. Persons in communal discernment work best when the steps are carefully outlined before the discernment process begins.

Schemel and Roemer outline seven essential elements, several of which may be conceived of as steps in a process. The precedent for their process is drawn from the experience of Ignatius of Loyola and his companions as they formed the Society of Jesus. While this represents a Roman Catholic view of spirituality, the method has been adapted and used by churches in the free church tradition. The essential elements include the following:

1) an explicit attitude and atmosphere of faith;

2) prayer before, during, and after for light and purification;

3) interior freedom: poised spiritual liberty;

4) information: disseminated, assimilated;

5) formulation of the Issue into a simple declarative sentence and the separation into con and pro reasons;

6) attempt at consensus; and

7) confirmation (congruence) in both the internal and the external.

In Schemel and Roemer's (p. 3f.) words:

The first three elements are habitual modes of mind and heart. They are part of the group's lifestyle rather than something it quickly does on the morning of a decision. The next three elements belong to the more formal part of the discernment process. The last element (congruence), is monitored in the group over time; even weeks, months, a year, as the new decision is worked out and tested.

Schemel and Roemer caution groups against trying to "form" or "forge" a consensus. Instead, the aim of the discernment process is to read the consensus that is already in the group. In contrast to Littell and other free church scholars cited earlier regarding the nature of group discussion, Schemel and Roemer make considerable room for resident (or designated) authority. They hold that when a group *cannot* or *will not* come to a consensus, the responsibility for making the decision rests with the designated authority. Perhaps this *modus operandi* reflects the more hierarchical nature of the Roman church than the more egalitarian nature of the free church.

Morris and Olsen offer yet another set of steps,[7] particularly adapted to large conferences comprising delegates from many churches. The process in their plan includes the formulation of a statement of direction, silent reflection, Bible study, sharing of stories, exploration and suggestions for improvement of possible options, weighing in on preferred solutions, determining the consensus, and closing the meeting.

SUMMARY

The free church is built on the concept of a voluntary community of believers which stands in contrast to the state church. The communal nature of the free church enables it to become a discerning group, drawing on the resources released by the Holy Spirit throughout the corporate body of believers. The heart of any discernment process in the church is to hear and respond to the will of God. This discernment is mandated and empowered by Jesus Christ as part of the nature and task of the church. Discernment generally involves a number of components and takes various forms, generally proceeding through a variety of steps or stages. Churches who cultivate the processes of prayerful discernment will be best equipped to interpret the Scriptures amid the community of God's people. That is the focus of the next chapter.

NOTES

1. See Schroeder (1988) for an explication of the binding and loosing function of the moral community.

2. Ross Bender, in his foreword to *Understanding Ministerial Leadership*, ed. John A. Esau, discusses the tensions within the Free Church community regarding the egalitarian nature of Christian ministry and the vocational "office" of pastoral ministry. He explains that particularly in the iconoclastic atmosphere of the 1960s, pastoral ministry was not adequately recognized and appreciated. Esau's book is a collection of essays which contribute to a developing theology of ministry which honors the pastoral office.

3. 1 Cor. 6:1-8 recounts a situation of conflict that existed between two members in the church. They went to law to settle it. Paul scolds the Corinthian Christians. He says they should have exercised discernment within the church itself. After all, Paul contends, Christians will one day judge angels. Shouldn't they be able to judge among themselves?

4. Schemel, along with Judith Roemer, led a large group of delegates in a discernment process regarding the church's response to church membership for persons with same-sex orientation. (See Minutes of March 11-14, 1999 Membership consultation 3)

5. Schemel and Roemer use thephrase *name of grace* to speak of the calling of an individual or group that figures largely in the discernment process.

6. Cf. Luke T. Johnson (1983, 1996) and Diettrich (1988).

7. The ten steps, briefly explained, are (1) *Framing*. This step involves the choice of a matter for discernment and a focus on how to approach it. (2) *Grounding*. To get the process started, a clear and concise statement will be drafted by the planning team and offered to the group. Small groups form "community" through storytelling and affirmation of the gifts individuals bring to the group. They also help to secure clarity about the way in which the group's values come to bear on the subject for discernment. (3) *Shedding*. Persons spend time in silent reflection—to name the baggage, investment, or passions each brings to the issue. They will be asked to consider what they will have to release so that the group can come to a state of indifference to anything but God's leading. Participants will also be asked to identify any unique concerns of the religious body they represent in anticipation that those concerns

may be laid aside and the group can come to corporate indifference. (4) *Rooting*. The plenary group makes biblical and historical connections with the matter to be discerned. Biblical scholars talk about the themes, images, and stories from biblical tradition, and pose questions for the small groups to consider. (5) *Listening*. The stories of individuals, congregations, or traditions are shared, although not as advocacy speeches. Small groups meet again to discuss the stories and to continue to explore the tradition. (6) *Exploring*. After quiet individual reflection and prayer, groups begin exploring the various paths that God may offer. Each group considers possible options. Options are shared with the larger group. (7) *Improving*. Options are offered to small groups for improvement. After a time of solitude, each person is invited to share how each path can be improved so that each is the best it can be. (8) *Weighing*. Participants remain in small groups. They are asked to be silent and to allow the Spirit to rest on each path. After silent prayer and reflection, group members report on where the Spirit has led them. (9) *Closing*. Each group leader tests for consensus or explores various ways to conclude the discernment. A person from each group may speak to the assembly of the wisdom of their group. This is not a debate but a sharing of wisdom. The method of concluding should have the approval of the assembly. (10) *Resting*. The moderator records the results of each step on the chart, seeking the consensus of the assembly.

CHAPTER 3

BIBLICAL INTERPRETATION IN THE ANABAPTIST TRADITION

ANABAPTIST HERMENEUTICS
IN HISTORICAL PERSPECTIVE

As progenitors of free church ideology, the Anabaptists of the sixteenth century promulgated a distinctive system of hermeneutics. Beginning in the late 1920s, Mennonite scholars published scholarly historical research on Anabaptist life and thought, including their unconventional approach to Scripture and its interpretation. Harold Bender of Goshen College led the way, founding the *Mennonite Quarterly Review* (*MQR*) in 1927.

Bender held that the Anabaptists rose from a common context in Zurich, Switzerland. He (1944) forged an identity between these ancestors and his own Mennonite Church, pleading for "Recovery of the Anabaptist Vision." Anabaptist historiography mushroomed, aided by the formation of the Mennonite Historical Archives and the pursuit of doctorates in history by a number of Mennonite scholars.

The uniqueness of Anabaptist hermeneutics, both in principle and in contrast to other Reformers, gradually came to the fore as part of the development of Anabaptist studies. Scholars from other church traditions, such as Stuart Murray of Baptist persuasion from the United Kingdom, have recently come to embrace an Anabaptist hermeneutic. Murray (2000, 10-12) gives eight reasons why Anabaptist perspectives on hermeneutics are recently gaining significance after years of minimal influence in the Christian world. Many "new" Anabaptists are finding that Anabaptist hermeneutics—born in the turbulence of theological change—provide a way to deal with the turbulence of theolocial change in the face of postmodernism. The current study provides brief references to a few studies devoted to Anabaptist hermeneutics, with a view to delineating the primary characteristics of sixteenth-century Anabaptist hermeneutics, particularly as they shed light on discernment within the hermeneutic community today.

Anabaptist Hermeneutics in the Context of the Protestant Reformation

Numerous Anabaptist scholars have attempted to delineate the essence of early Anabaptist hermeneutics.[1] To some extent, this involves comparison and contrast with their Protestant challengers. John Roth, current editor of the *MQR* (1994, 36) asserts that Anabaptists held similar views of Scripture as the major Reformers: They differed from other Protestants primarily regarding the question of "*how* the truths of Scripture were to be interpreted and applied."

Stuart Murray, in a major study of early Anabaptist hermeneutics, explains that Anabaptists differed from their contemporaries regarding the value of theological study vis-a-vis a simple biblicism. The major Reformers, for example, favored systematic theology as opposed to biblical theology. Thus, they tended to combine theology and biblical interpretation, as did Augustine. In this vein, they argued that Scripture must be understood in light of doctrines such as justification by faith. The Anabaptist rejected this approach, believing that it set doctrine above Scripture and resulted in "a blinkered approach to the Scriptures" (Murray 1992, 78).

In a later study that attempted to capture the bare essential of radical Anabaptist faith, Murry (2010, 45) argues that

We are committed to a Jesus-centered approach to the
Bible, and to the community of faith as the primary context in which we read the Bible and discern and apply its
implications for discipleship. This approach elevates discipleship and community above the doctrines promulgated by the magisterial church.

Despite differences, the Anabaptists shared areas of agreement with such major Reformers as Luther, Calvin, and
Zwingli. They agreed, for example, on the "commitment to the
'plain sense' of Scripture; emphasizing the right of all believers
to read, discuss and interpret Scripture; refusing to let biblical
interpretation be governed by ecclesiastical traditions; and concern with the literal sense of texts rather than allegorical meanings" (Murray, 1992, 43). Sometimes, however, Anabaptists accused the Reformers of applying principles inconsistently.

The Reformers insisted on the right of all to interpret the
Bible for themselves. But, as Murray (1992, 47-48) contends,

three inter-connected reservations were imposed on this
right of private interpretation: first, conclusions reached
by private individuals should agree with those taught by
accredited church leaders; second, scholarship was important in attaining a correct understanding; and third,
there was an emphasis on the need to read the original languages in which the Bible had been written.

The result of imposing these limitations, according to
the Anabaptists, was that interpretation had been liber-
ated from the monopoly of the Pope and priests only to be
subjected to the monopoly of preachers and scholars.

J. Denny Weaver contends (118-9) that

While the Protestant Reformers tended to retain the right
of interpretation for the authoritative teachers, Anabaptists put the Bible in the hands of laypersons and involved
every member in interpretation by making the believing
community of voluntary members the locus of interpretation.

This practice is the essence of the hermeneutic community as
discussed below.

Frits Kuiper proposes that despite all the diversity among
Anabaptist groups, "there was an essential agreement as to the

manner of understanding the Bible" (115).

> Their biblicism possessed a candor and a simplicity that, according to them, was normal. Nevertheless, this was not common among the Christians of that generation nor of any other generation since the apostolic age. (116-7)

Although he sees areas of agreement with other Reformers, Roth (52-3) discusses six distinguishing features of early Anabaptist hermeneutics. They are numbered and summarized below:

1) The meaning of Scripture was clear, even to the unlearned. All points of confusion or apparent contradiction in Scripture could be clarified by Scripture itself, that is, by reference to other biblical passages rather than to private revelation or tradition.

2) The life and teachings of Jesus offered an important key to unlocking the mysteries of the written word. All of Scripture, both the Old and New Testaments, needed to be interpreted in a way that was consistent with the revelation of God in Jesus Christ.

3) A simple and literal obedience to the clear commands of Scripture, particularly the teachings of Jesus, was inextricably linked to a life of faithful obedience.

4) A distinction was made between the Old Testament (covenant, promise, warfare) and the New Testament (grace, fulfillment, suffering love). Particularly in their teaching on the oath and the sword, the Anabaptists granted to the latter an authority superior to that of the Old Testament.

5) God speaks both in the Outer (or written) word of Scripture as well as in the Inner (or spiritual) word of revelation. Both are necessary for a proper understanding of God's will, but either one could easily be stressed to the detriment of the other. The Anabaptists sought to balance the Outer word and the Inner word.

6) Scripture is best interpreted as a communal process, in the context of a body of believers who, with the help of the Holy Spirit, gather to study God's Word and to discern God's will.

While Roth's summary captures the essence of Anabaptist hermeneutics, I shall attempt, in this next section of the study, to paint, in short broad strokes, my own summary of the early

Anabaptist consensus regarding an interpretive approach to Scripture.

Primary Characteristics of Anabaptist Hermeneutics

An emphasis on Christ

A key principle of Anabaptist biblical interpretation was christocentric focus. Murray (1992) says it well:

> Menno [Simons], like Hubmaier, was confident that the words and example of Jesus were clear and straightforward by comparison with other parts of Scripture. Indeed, he risked consigning some texts to the scrap heap because he regarded them as contradicting what Christ taught. (107)

As Murray (1992) shows, in his reply to Gellius Faber, Menno said that he followed "'Christ's plain word and command, the doctrine and usage of the holy apostles in the first, unfalsified church.' Here the link between Christocentrism and the Anabaptist commitment to the clarity and simplicity of Scripture becomes explicit" (107).

Anabaptists agreed with Luther, Melanchthon, and others that the christological principle was the hermeneutical key that would open every passage of Scripture. But for the Reformers, *christological* referred primarily to the work of Christ and the principle of justification by faith. For the Anabaptists, "Christocentrism was tied more firmly to the human Jesus than was the Reformers' christological approach" (Murray, 1992, 129).

Anabaptists viewed Jesus differently than the Reformers on a number of fronts. They focused on the person of Jesus Christ rather than a doctrine based on his saving actions; they emphasized the humanity of the historical Jesus; and they were more willing than the Reformers to accept Jesus' deeds and words as normative. Further, they extended Christocentrism to embrace the whole of the New Testament, with a concurrent emphasis on the cruciality of a life-experience of the living Christ as a prerequisite for interpretation, a prerequisite that no amount of education could replace (Murray, 1992, 129).

Anabaptist hermeneutics were "Christocentric in methodology as well as in content" (Murray, 1992, 113). A first step in hermeneutics, then, was to ask how Jesus would interpret a passage. As a result, christocentric hermeneutics meant for Anabaptists that some passages of Scripture had greater authority than others. The sayings of Jesus eventually became a "canon within the canon."

Perhaps in reaction to Catholic, Lutheran, and Reformed teachings about Christ's uniqueness as a mediator between God and humankind, Anabaptists may sometimes have overemphasized Jesus as a model for present-day believers. With their strong emphasis on the humanity of Jesus, they may have failed to see the hermeneutical implications of Jesus' divinity. In Murray's judgment, some Anabaptist writings confuse aspects of Jesus' life which related to his redemptive function with aspects that can properly be imitated by his followers (1992, 140). Some aspects of Jesus' life defy contemporary analogy.

An emphasis on the church

The nature and function of Anabaptist biblical interpretation was at least partly shaped by their distinctive ecclesiology. Murray (1992) goes so far as to say that the Anabaptists were "ecclesiocentric" in their biblical interpretation. That is, they believed that any interpretation should be judged by its usefulness to the congregation, particularly since they believed they were in faithful continuity with the early church.

The Dutch believers in seventeenth-century Holland can serve as an example of an ecclesiocentric approach, particularly as it relates to church discipline. As Douglas Shantz (198-9) observes:

> Dirk's hermeneutical views on the respective functions of the Holy Spirit and the written Word, and on the relation of the two testaments, can be properly understood only in the context of his concern for establishing a pure believers church based on the use of the ban. This ecclesiological concern served as a presupposition to shape and govern his understanding and application of the Scriptures. Because Dirk's hermeneutical views were influenced by this one dominating practical concern, his interpretation is best viewed as "a hermeneutic of the pure Church," in contrast to the hermeneutics of Spiritualist individualism, of the Munster Kingdom or of the magisterial state church.

Shantz continues: "Dirk . . . saw two kinds of preaching and two ways of using the Scriptures: preaching of 'the letter,' which was ineffective, and preaching 'by the impulse of the Holy Spirit,' by which the Word became powerful in bearing fruit" (204-5). "It was the distinction of the false teacher that he preached the Word in such a way that it failed to manifest its characteristic power to change lives" (205). As explained above, the heart of the Anabaptist view of the church was a redeemed community of disciples who manifested the power of the risen Christ in their lives. In this vein, Shantz contends:

Dirk desired a proper hermeneutical foundation on the issue of Word and Spirit to support his whole vision of a restored New Testament community of believers, based on New Testament concepts of holiness and the ban. Otherwise he feared that Anabaptism would fade into either moral decadence (a reform apart from the Spirit) or the scattered individualism of the Spiritualists (a reform apart from the New Testament's model of community). His own brother Obbe had been lost to the Spiritualists, partly because of Franck's persuasion. This fact added a note of practical immediacy to what otherwise might appear to have been merely an intellectual issue of hermeneutics. (206)

Shantz (206) summarizes:

Dirk's hermeneutic has distinguished itself as one, if not the only one, perfectly suited to the kind of restitution he envisioned. Here lies the true significance of his approach [to biblical interpretation]. Doubtless other factors played a part in causing Dirk to understand and use the Scriptures as he did. But we have sought to show that for Dirk it was impossible to read the Scriptures without having in mind the fundamental ecclesiological and practical concerns that the Scriptures serve.

Because Anabaptists believed that the congregation was a factor in determining the correctness of any interpretation, the "congregation both shaped and was shaped by the way in which Scripture was interpreted to produce a congregation that was true to their understanding of biblical ecclesiology" (Murray 1992, 236). This approach illustrates one form of the hermeneutical circle, in which the pre-understanding or pre-disposition one brings to Scripture as a whole influences one's understanding of particular Scripture texts, and vice-versa. When Anabaptists looked for particular texts to undergird their own view of the church, their approach may have smacked of utilitarianism or pragmatism.

Anabaptist emphasis on the pure church frequently led to tensions and schism, often revolving around questions of church discipline. "Opinions differed about the relationship between the newfound freedom from the Catholic hierarchy and the need to maintain an orderly, distinct congregation" (Weaver, 106). As Weaver explains, "The first unsolvable crisis relating to discipline produced not only a schism within the Dutch movement, but also led to a break in relations between Dutch and South German Anabaptists." Weaver observes that "The long-term result of . . . exchanges between the Dutch Mennonites and the South German Anabaptists led the way in having the southerners banned and their baptism no longer accepted as valid" (107). An ecclesiocentric approach, then, can lead to excessive provincialism.

Reliance on the Spirit

The Anabaptists of the sixteenth century were the "charismatics" of their day. They continually emphasized reliance on the Spirit for understanding of Scripture, so that it might rightly be called a hermeneutical principle. Reflecting on Anabaptist teaching, Franklin Littell (90) asserts that under the guidance of the Holy Spirit, God people are called to "arrive at and hold the disciplines which truly reflect the will of God as understood by the whole Church of all nations and all generations. But God's Word and Will is not simply to be found in timeless truths or speculative systems." Rather, it comes at the "point of choice," to specific people at specific times in specific places. This highlights the need for "common study, common prayer, and fraternal discussion among co-believers."

Murray echoes this sentiment. He believes that for Anabaptists, "reliance on the Spirit applied to *understanding* Scripture, not just responding to it, and that the Spirit was expected to guide interpreters actively rather than simply through their reasoning ability and hard work (Murray, 1992, 202).

The Anabaptists accused the Reformers of equating the Holy Spirit with human reasoning. "The Reformers spoke about the Holy Spirit, but the Anabaptists were unconvinced that the Spirit was allowed to operate in the state churches" (Murray 199,: 202). "As a charismatic but biblical movement, they were committed to a 'pneumatic exegesis' of Scripture" (Murray 1992, 205). Therefore, "reliance on the Spirit was preferred to reliance on education and scholarship" (208). It was this emphasis on the Spirit's activity in the church which differentiated Anabaptist hermeneutics from other sixteenth-century options" (Murray, 1992, 212-13).

However, Murray warns: "Various aberrations and extreme practices that plagued early Anabaptism demonstrate the risks involved in encouraging believers to rely on the Spirit's guidance in interpreting Scripture" (1992, 212). As noted above, both spiritualism and textualism are barriers to discernment; they are also barriers to proper biblical interpretation.

While Anabaptism offered various perspectives on the issue of Word and Spirit, the contribution of the movement as a whole was to provide a "mediating alternative to the Reformers, who seemed to give inadequate room to the Spirit, and to the Spiritualists who seemed to give inadequate room to the Word" (Murray, 1992, 223). Tugged in both directions by their contemporaries, the Anabaptists eventually found a middle way.

Orientation toward the New Testament

Unlike their Protestant contemporaries, Anabaptists drew fairly sharp distinctions between the New Testament and the Old. As Murray states: "For Menno, literal adherence to Old Testament texts carried a connotation of disobedience, unlike the New Testament where the opposite was true" (1992, 174). "The New Testament was to be interpreted literally, because it was the reality, the essence, the fulfillment. The Old Testament was to be interpreted spiritually because its literal sense, though still historically important, was inapplicable" (1992, 175).

Anabaptists generally saw a discontinuity between the saving acts of God in the Old Testament and those depicted in the New. The Reformers saw much more continuity. Yet Anabaptists used the Old Testament in a number of important ways: 1) as a "secondary source of authority when it was perceived to agree with the New Testament"; 2) "it was used devotionally as a source of encouragement, comfort and inspiration"; 3) "it was valued as vital preparation for the coming of Christ and the new covenant"; 4) it "was regarded as having continuing authority 'outside the perfection of Christ,' as a guide for the ordering of society"; 5) they drew from Catholic, Protestant, spiritualistic, and rationalist sources to assimilate "otherwise incongruent parts of the Old Testament" (Murray 1992, 166-70).

In regard to the Anabaptist practice of favoring the New Testament over the Old, Werner Packull has suggested that until 1529 the Old Testament was not widely available for lay Bible study in the vernacular. This alone may have influenced their theological leanings (42). Because few Anabaptists were capable of studying the original languages, they relied on biblical translations that were just emerging at that time. Particularly influential were Erasmus' notations on baptism in a current translation of the gospel of Matthew.

Some Anabaptist scholars conclude that the Anabaptists went too far in their belief that the New superseded the Old. So Murray (1992, 182-3) concludes:

> The task of contemporary interpreters is to develop a methodology for interpreting the Old Testament that is faithful to the important Anabaptist perspectives on ecclesiology and ethics but that values the Old Testament and is consistent with the essential unity between the Testaments, which the Anabaptists themselves strove, but to some extent failed, to maintain.

The church as a hermeneutic community

This study maintains that Anabaptists believed that the Scripture could best be interpreted in community. In his in-depth study of Anabaptist approaches to hermeneutic community, Murray (1992) asserts that

> Designating the local congregation as the locus of interpretation was arguably the most important and distinctive Anabaptist contribution to sixteenth-century hermeneutics. The interpreting community was the focal point of

Anabaptist hermeneutics, the context for the hermeneutical enfranchisement of every believer, and the setting for the reliance on the Holy Spirit. (420)

Murray continues, "Individuals were not to rely on their own understandings, nor to discount the contributions of brothers and sisters. The ideal Anabaptist interpreter was a Spirit-led believer-in-community" (Murray 1992, 95). Of course, as Murray (1992, 224) notes, "the term *hermeneutic community* was not used by Anabaptists. It is a scholarly definition of the role of their congregations in interpreting Scripture."

"The Anabaptists were committed to the right of all believers to read and interpret Scripture," Murray points out, "but from the movement's earliest years their understanding of community was so strong that it was unthinkable that this right should be exercised in isolation or not be subject to testing in congregational meetings" (1992, 226). Murray sees this as a "middle way between rampant individualism and a restrictive hierarchical [Catholic] model." This required a congregation of committed believers "eager to obey Scripture and open to the Spirit." According to Murray (1992, 229), such congregations were virtually nonexistent in the state churches.

"The congregation's task was not to count hands [to determine a majority or minority voice]," underscores Murray, "but to discern through whom the Spirit was speaking. Only within a congregation that perceived itself to be a charismatic community could this kind of consensus decision-making be practiced" (Murray 1992, 214). He concludes that "The hermeneutic community was arguably the most radical and significant aspect of Anabaptist hermeneutics" (1992, 218).

Murray (1992, 240-1) asserts that the leaders in these congregations functioned more like umpires than sole participants in Bible teaching. By choosing leaders from among the congregations, the churches put less importance on formal training in Bible study. In fact, they tended to denigrate formal training in the Scriptures. While there were professionals among the early Anabaptists, few of them were trained in theology. It appears that they were highly suspicious of supposed experts in theology. They believed that every sincere Christian should be allowed to interpret the Scriptures, lest the dominance of popes and bishops be replaced by the dominance of scholars.

"It was Hubmaier who argued most vigorously for the principle of the hermeneutic community," reports Roth, "insisting that the honest, spirit-inspired reading of Scripture by simple lay folk offered a better understanding of the will of God than the scholarly treatises of the learned" (41). This seems ironic, since "Hubmaier possessed the only doctor's degree among all the first-generation Anabaptists" (Weaver, 3).

Although he raises some questions about the actual practice of hermeneutic community, Roth (61-2) asserts that

> the notion of active congregational involvement in biblical exegesis seems to have been a persistent ideal within the groups that descended from the Anabaptists and that ideal continued to provide a source of ferment and renewal in a wide variety of contexts and circumstances.

That ideal, assumed in these pages, can serve as an inspiration and a model for contemporary interpretation in the church. As hinted above, however, Anabaptist scholars have some reservations about the popular conceptions of Anabaptist hermeneutics, including their approach to communal hermeneutics.

Revisionist Critiques Regarding Anabaptist Hermeneutics

Modern scholars have offered revisionist notions, both of the popular history of Anabaptism and of Anabaptist practice. For example, John Howard Yoder (1957), a prominent interpreter of Anabaptist history and theology, argues that Harold Bender attributed too much continuity between early Anabaptists and modern Mennonites. And sociologist Cal Redekop is less committed than the early historians to some ideal drawn from Anabaptism. He argues that Anabaptists tended to see the world through the lenses of an extremely sectarian world view. The world was divided into two classes; their dualism was clearly stated in Article Four of their Confession at Schleitheim.

This sharp dualism, if embraced today, hardly allows for objective study of history. It may even lead to making one's own history normative for all time. In Rodney Sawatsky's words, "Sectarian perfectionism and the 'scientific' history which helped in eroding the Anabaptist vision are at fundamental odds. They cannot survive together!" (12).

The revisionist turn in Anabaptist historiography made a case for polygenetic Anabaptist origins spawned by diverse causes. The new view was quickly adopted; most contemporary Anabaptist historians do not believe in a monogenetic Anabaptism. Some historians have pointed out the close relationship between the social situation of the peasants and the theology of the Anabaptists. Might the separatist nature of the Swiss Brethren have its roots in the failure of the Peasants' War? Might the "priesthood of all believers" have risen from the anticlericalism of the times? Might the Anabaptist rejection of the tithe be linked to the encumbrance of the tithe around Zurich to support the state church? (See Roth, 43).

In the same vein, as a social historian, Roth (36) raises questions about the earlier scholarly consensus regarding Anabaptist hermeneutics. His understanding of their approach to Scripture is "more sensitive to the diversity within the Anabaptist movement," believes Roth, "more careful to distinguish between stated principles and actual practice, and more attuned to the broader social, political and economic context within which discussions about biblical interpretation occurred." Roth (38) reminds readers that "Anabaptism was a diverse, even fragmented movement, characterized by deep hostility and divisions within and among various groups."

Particularly in the case of the Swiss Brethren and Hutterites, agreed-upon hermeneutical principles didn't yield a common mind on many theological questions. Yet traditional approaches to Anabaptist hermeneutics have glossed over or lost this perspective of differences between groups.

> Roth insists that the principles of Anabaptist hermeneutics were salient, not because they resolved all exegetical questions. To the contrary, embedded within each of the basic hermeneutical principles were fundamental tensions—in some cases outright contradictions—that led almost inevitably to disagreement and to varying understandings as to how these tensions might be resolved. (60)

Perhaps "the Anabaptist use of Scripture can be best described not as a set of fixed, normative hermeneutical principles," Roth (44) suggests, "but rather as a series of arguments or debates into which participants were drawn precisely because they agreed upon the importance of the issue being debated." This frame of reference points to a dynamic model for understanding the factors that drew "the spiritual ancestors of the Mennonites and Brethren into a common conversation, though not always a common mind (46-7)."

Roth (40) observes that the idea of a "hermeneutical community" has been championed by John Howard Yoder as a primary motif of Anabaptist hermeneutics. But Roth asks, "How consistently did the Swiss Brethren—or any other Anabaptist group—actually implement the ideal of a 'hermeneutical community'"? Murray asserts that there are few examples of the hermeneutic community operating in practice. While scholars point to Schleitheim (where a confession of faith was written) as a case in point of communal discernment, this says little about how congregations functioned in actuality. Menno Simons does not seem to have practiced it consistently. And the Hutterite brothers soon developed a powerful hierarchy which hewed to traditional interpretation.

It is unclear *how* the idea of the hermeneutical community took shape in Anabaptist congregations. Beyond Schleitheim, there are few other examples of translocal communities. Gatherings at Teufen and Augsburg the year after Schleitheim seemed to employ similar concepts of communal hermeneutics as that used in local churches. However, when Anabaptist groups disagreed, there was no hierarchy to enforce a particular biblical interpretation. As a result, various groups "resorted to excommunicating *en masse* other groups with whom they disagreed" (Murray, 1992, 248).

Further, Roth (42) argues, while Anabaptists were said to be biblicists or literalists, there is much evidence to show that they depended on a variety of extra-biblical sources (confessions of faith, letters, hymnody, martyr stories, etc.) that served effectively as a "canon within a canon." So

> an insistence on Anabaptist literalism as a principle separating them from Catholics and Protestants overshadows the ways in which elements of tradition, creed, charisma and the authority of office also shaped the Anabaptist reading of Scripture in decisive ways.

Murray (1992, 318) also believes that Anabaptist hermeneutics were definitely shaped by the ecclesiological changes taking place at that crucial juncture in history, just as current hermeneutics are being shaped by the changes in the global church community today.

Historian C. Arnold Snyder (382) insists that to be Anabaptist today is to have received a well-defined canon within a canon. He asserts that "it will no longer do to operate under the fiction that the believers church tradition is 'purely biblical' whereas other readings of Scripture are tainted with 'human tradition.'" Snyder is convinced that "The believers church reading of Scripture is also a human tradition." Further, Snyder (383) attests that the early predisposition to lay interpretation, which he calls "pneumatic democracy," was short-lived. It gave way early to a "growing emergence of a tradition of textual interpretations" that "looked to elders and bishops" for "definitive interpretations." The interpretive ground was not as level as depicted by popular visions of Anabaptism.

Steve Dintaman, Dale Schrag, Walter Klassen, and A. James Reimer have all rendered scholarly critiques of the Anabaptist vision of hermeneutics. Each believes that Anabaptism cannot legitimately be made a "canon within the canon" lest it become a heresy. Rather, each asserts that we must first affirm what is common with trinitarian Christian theology, then consider Anabaptism's hermeneutical principles (Sawatsky).

Murray (1992, 290-1) enumerates seven shortcomings of Anabaptist hermeneutics:

1) They drove too large a wedge between understanding and application;

2) without proper understanding of Scripture, their application and activism may have been harmful rather than fruitful;

3) better synthesis between action and reflection would have increased their understanding;

4) they may have underestimated the subtlety of their own human sin influencing their interpretation;

5) they tended to see falsehood rather than ignorance as the main enemy;

6) their prior ethical commitments may have skewed their interpretation of the ethical demands of the gospel; and

7) their focus on ethics may have prevented them from meeting the living Christ.

Murray goes on to argue that Anabaptist communal hermeneutics had several limitations that "must be addressed if the full potential of congregational hermeneutics is to be realized." They are summarized briefly here: "First, the hermeneutic community need not exclude scholars, nor need scholars operate outside hermeneutic communities" (1992, 424).

"Second, the hermeneutic community need not exclude those who have studied Scripture in earlier generations" (Murray 1992, 424).

> Third, the hermeneutic community should include interpreters from diverse social, political and cultural backgrounds. A potential weakness of the local congregation operating as the hermeneutic community is that its presuppositions may be unrecognized and it may interpret Scripture in ways that merely confirm its existing convictions. (Murray, 1992, 426)

This is a form of the hermeneutical spiral that can become a vicious circle. Since most communities assume themselves to be faithful, they interpret the Scripture in light of their understanding of faithfulness, simply reinforcing their own concepts. A safeguard from this tendency is some translocal expression of the hermeneutical community.

"Fourth, the ecclesiological shape of the hermeneutic community should not be unduly circumscribed." In other words, "such a model may not be identified exclusively with a local congregation" (Murray, 1992, 427).

> A crucial element is size: the community must be small enough for personal accountability to be realistic and for consensus to be reached, or else crucial features of the hermeneutic community model cannot operate and there will be reversion to individualistic and institutional hermeneutics. (Murray, 1992, 428)

Anabaptist scholars continue to find inspiration, identity, and direction in the example of their sixteenth century faith ancestors. As the same time, revisionist scholars have critiqued traditional conceptions of Anabaptist hermeneutics. Over the past few decades, many new influences have shaped the way that scholars both conceive of the church and its hermeneutical task. These influences are the focus of the next section.

MODERN DEVELOPMENTS INFLUENCING CURRENT ANABAPTIST HERMENEUTICS

The Socio-Religious Effects of Modernization

Led by insights from sociological study, scholars from various disciplines have attempted to trace the effects of industrialization and technological development on human societies, generally under the rubric of modernization or secularization.[2] The changes in the modern world, particularly since the invention of steam power, have profoundly shaped human consciousness. The recent emergence of electronic, computer, and Internet technology have rapidly disseminated ideas which represent competing *realities* and new ways of knowing. Religious establishments, once the dominant force in many societies, now find their scope of influence vastly reduced. Religious assumptions about the nature of the supernatural are increasingly under attack.

Social theorists have sometimes depicted modernization as a seemingly unstoppable march toward technological determinism and secularization of religion. But this is not necessarily so.[3] Marsha Witten argued that religious groups may respond to the forces of modernization through accommodation, resistance, or reflexive reframing. And James Hunter (134-5) observed that the conditions of modernity sometimes spawn cycles of religious upsurge and conservatism in an attempt to harness modernity's unruly and unkind forces.[4] Further, "a body of theory suggests that there is a point in the modernization process when large numbers of people began to feel adrift and to seek more rigid forms of authority and order" (Toews, 1983, 256).

Meanwhile Nancy Ammerman shows that the tensions between liberalizing and conserving religious ideologies may produce intense religious battles. The fundamentalist-modernist debate in the early 1900s, for example, was a protracted battle that drew Mennonite scholars into the mist of the fray. It eventuated in the temporary closing of Goshen College, a Mennonite school that was perceived as being too modernistic.

Along with other denominations in the free church tradition, the Mennonite Church today finds itself torn between two opposing religious camps of relatively equal size, with increasing hostility toward each other.[5] In Wuthnow's (1989, *Struggle*, 22) terms, one comprises a predominance of *evangelicals, fundamentalists*, and *religious conservatives*; the other has a predominance of *religious liberals, humanists*, and *secularists*. In general, liberals emphasize the behavioral aspects of religion accompanied by political activism, while conservatives emphasize the value dimensions of religion, along with personal morality.

Higher education tends to create social and cultural distinctions, and reinforces the split between the two groups. There is a growing polarity between the educated, who typically advocate more relativistic social positions and more engagement on social issues, and the less educated, who typically hold more traditional beliefs and focus on personal morality (Wuthnow, 1989, *Struggle*, 16). The Kauffman and Driedger (1991) social survey of Mennonites showed clear correlations between higher education and more liberal beliefs.

The division between liberals and conservatives does not fall neatly along denominational lines. Rather, the lines divide denominations and congregations, even groupings as intimate as family and small group fellowships. At times, there are more differences *within* the Mennonite church than between Mennonites and persons of other denominations. One study indicated that, unlike other kinds of prejudice and hostility, ill feelings regarding theology did not mitigate between these two groups as they came into more contact with each other.

Despite their basic teaching on the ethic of love and forgiveness, there have been many acrimonious interchanges, even between moderate and conservative Christians (Ammerman). Differing methods of biblical interpretation or differing views of the Bible[6] are often the flashpoint in the disputes that surround moral issues such as the ordination of women or the reception into church membership of persons with same-sex orientation or partnerships.

Modernization, higher education, and increasing theological sophistication have transformed the way modern Anabaptists read the Bible and discern its meaning for their lives. Until this century, adherents in the Anabaptist tradition tended to interpret the Scriptures at face value, as though God were speaking directly to them in the text. The historical and rhetorical exigencies of the situation that prompted the writing of particular biblical texts were largely suppressed. The introduction of historical critical studies has served to bring increasing sophistication to the task of Bible study, with increasing awareness of the gulf between the ancient and contemporary worlds. In concert with other forms of modern criticism, it has also served to increase the gulf between those who approach the text in differing ways.

Historical-Critical Study of Scripture

Several volumes of essays on hermeneutics by Anabaptist scholars point to a dramatic shift in methods of Bible study over the past several decades. Anabaptists now call into service the methods of modern historiography and literary criticism for determining the social context, exigencies of production, and meaning of the biblical text. A few examples of scholarly work, all based in Mennonite seminaries, will suffice. Klassen and Snyder's (1962) volume contains essays employing the principles of historical-critical methodology in New Testament studies.

Willard Swartley's (1984) edited volume *Essays on Biblical Interpretation: Anabaptist-Mennonite Perspectives* and Swartley and Koontz's (1987) *Perspectives on Feminist Hermeneutics* address the questions of hermeneutics in direct fashion. Perry Yoder's (1982) eight-step guide to Bible study includes the extensive use of historical-critical tools for discovering the original meaning of a text, the principles embodied in the text, and the use of analogy to bridge the gap between the worlds of the author and the reader. Lydia Harder (1987) and (1998) explores Mennonite-Feminist hermeneutics in the context of the Anabaptist hermeneutic community and emphasis on obedience and discipleship. And Paul Zehr's *Biblical Criticism in the Life of the Church* offers suggestions for the incorporation of critical studies in the life of the church.

Swartley (1983, 244) believes historical critical studies have had positive value for the church, "vastly expanding our knowledge of the historical, cultural, and linguistic backgrounds of the Bible." His comments reflect the common modern perception that a foundational task of the biblical scholar is to discover the author's original intent. Nevertheless, he asserts that "in its most critical form and by itself, the historical-critical method is inadequate" (219). In response, he offers a number of guidelines as suggestions for Bible study (245).

Not all Anabaptists are convinced that there is room for historical-critical study. In recent generations conservative resistance has coalesced into such groups as the Fellowship of Concerned Mennonites or the Evangelical Anabaptist Fellowship. The tools of higher criticism are anathema to such groups, for whom biblical interpretation approaches are a core concern.

While embracing critical methods of Bible study, Marlin Miller also discusses their relativizing nature, contending that "judgments of probability" arise from consideration of the evidence, assessed by the "norms of critical reason" rather than "traditional authority." Probability, rather than certainty, marks the conclusions of contemporary biblical scholarship. "Criticism as a stance cannot and does not intend to claim the kind of certainty presupposed by the traditional dogmatic method of theology" (225-6).

Implications for biblical interpretation in the hermeneutic community quickly come to the fore. The stance of doubt introduced by critical studies may function in the community of faith either as a welcome relief from dogmatic oppression or an assault on faith and obedience to Scripture. The need for careful discernment is manifest.

New Theories of Biblical Translation

Along with modernization in thought and its accompanying pluralism has come the realization that language is both an expression and shaper of culture. Missionaries equipped with the tools of cultural anthropology have attempted to translate the Scriptures from the original languages into the modern tongues and dialects of tribes and nations in even the remotest corners of the globe.[7] At home, too, members of the church have access to a growing number of Bible versions.

Recent years have seen the printing of a plethora of Bible translations, reflecting various theories of translation, from literal or formal equivalence to free paraphrases. In recent years, translators have applied the concept of "dynamic equivalence," a three-step process involving 1) biblical exegesis, 2) transference of the meaning by analogy to contemporary concepts, and 3) the generation of an equivalent expression in modern language. Although the immensely popular *New International Version* of the Bible employs the method of dynamic equivalence, this theory has come under increasing scrutiny by conservatives in recent years,[8] particularly as the editors of the *NIV* sought to make further revisions.

Translations deal in differing ways with grammar and syntax, the translation of proper names, euphemisms, specialized or idiomatic expressions, as well as concepts having to do with measurement (time, weight, distance, height, money). But the most controversial issue in modern biblical translation theory is the portrayal of gender in the text.[9] In an attempt to be "gender accurate," several recent versions and translations have employed gender-neutral language unless the use of specifically male or female language is deliberately called for in the text. These versions/translations are dubbed as "inclusive-language" texts.[10] At stake in the inclusive-language controversy are deeply held beliefs about the roles of men and women in the home, church, and society.

The advent of many available translations has had its effect on biblical interpretation in the congregation. At any given time, congregants may have in hand several different Bible translations. In the context of discernment regarding the meaning or application of a given passage of Scripture in the church, persons will rely on the translations available to them. When the available translations present different meanings or indicate variants in original manuscripts, the historical exigencies in the production or transmission of the texts is brought to the forefront. An element of doubt may replace the certainty which accompanied the use of a single standard text. As a result, the sense of biblical authority, with an attendant call to obedience, may be compromised.

The use of free translations (or paraphrases) may make it particularly difficult for free churches with a hermeneutics of obedience to enforce literal adherence to biblical directives. For example, some conservative Anabaptist groups practice the Holy Kiss, or Christian Salutation, as a scriptural ordinance for believers in every age to keep.[11] But new paraphrases of the

Scriptures indicate that a handshake or warm embrace, rather than a kiss, is an appropriate gesture of Christian love.[12] At the very least, such new versions highlight the cultural distance between the biblical and contemporary worlds and invite reflection on the cultural relativity of all New Testament commands.

Insights from the Sociology of Knowledge

Modern theorists have explored the relationship between social life and human thought. Therefore, Anabaptist scholars are increasingly aware that ideas do not simply pass from one individual to another; they are mediated through social structures. Through the sharing of ideas and other means of influence, powerful people help to shape social structures, which in turn shape ideas. While there is no simple causal relationship, we must pay attention to the "environmental resources used in ideological production" (Wuthnow, 1989, *Communities*, 17).[13]

Building on earlier theories of the social base for knowledge, Berger and Luckmann (1967) argue that social structure and social consciousness are dialectically interrelated. They propose that socially determined structures undergird social actors' world views and understanding of what is real; that *reality* of everyday life is socially constructed and maintained. According to Berger and Luckmann's theory, ideas become and remain plausible only in the context of particular social situations or *plausibility structures*.[14] This theory suggests that the dialectic of social life and thought involves the interaction of three processes: externalization, objectivation, and internalization (Berger and Luckmann).[15]

Externalization is the active process by which the social world is produced, created, shaped, and modified. This part of the processes focuses on humans as the producers of reality. It is an *everyday* reality, based on observations and experiences of human life. This social reality is encapsulated in a *symbolic universe*. The world of words is used to express these observations and experiences, defining life *as it really is*. They construct the world view that is passed on to the next generation.

Objectivation is the institutionalization of ideas and reality. This reality is antecedent and external to those who live under its influence, especially the young. This reality cannot be avoided; it must be taken into account by those who want to live successfully in a given social situation. The human and social authorship of the ideas and beliefs fades into the background as new generations take the shared social reality for granted. Language is the most powerful and coercive means by which society imposes its definition of reality upon human actors.

Internalization is the process by which individual consciousness is shaped by the objectified reality of the group; objective facts becomes subjective reality. This process is most evident and influential in the socialization and rearing of the young. Through the process of internalization, the society's definitions and meanings become the individual's personal meanings and convictions. While persons may grow up to experience secondary internalization, an earlier stage leaves the deepest marks. Part of this process is language acquisition; the first language shapes reality the most deeply. Perhaps this is why it is called *the mother tongue*.

Specific institutions and institutional processes are the carriers for specific structures of consciousness; they help produce the specific social circumstances that make particular modes of conociousnoss believable. According to Berger and Luckmann, the religious sect is the prototypical subsociety which limits membership to those who share a similar reality. As Emerson said succinctly: "If I know your sect, I anticipate your argument" (quoted in Ruth, 2). Within the sheltering community of the sect, conceptions of reality which deviate wildly from that of broader society may be maintained.

Until the late nineteenth century, Mennonites lived for the most part in sect-like communities. These communities provided the social structure necessary to maintain their distinctive ideology, based on two-kingdom theology (cf. Roy Roth). In essence, this theology reflected an all-encompassing ideological dualism. Friedmann went so far as to declare this dualism the essence of early Anabaptism.

For the first several centuries of their existence, Mennonites (particularly the Swiss-German branch) lived by an ethical code based on two-kingdom theology expressed in the complementary doctrines of nonresistance and nonconformity. These doctrines seemed to be firmly based in the plausibility structures of the sect-like Mennonite social community; few other Christian communions interpreted the Scripture in ways that supported such radical applications about the church's relationship to the state.[16]

However, various modernizing factors led to the breakup of Mennonite communities. Alternative service programs such as Civilian Public Service (CPS), Voluntary Service (VS), and I-W service, for example, drew large numbers of young Mennonites out of their home communities. When individual Mennonites left the farms and moved into cities, they encountered new social structures. Consequently, they began to adopt new ways of thinking.

As Mennonites made their way up in the world, they also encountered new ideas in the academies of higher learning. Social theory in the academy has been particularly impacted by two social movements in contemporary life, liberation theology and feminist hermeneutics. Both movements have made a considerable impact on biblical interpretation in the twentieth century. Both have their roots in Marxist social theory.

Karl Marx , one of the most influential social theorists of modern times, explored the relationship between ideology and class structure, particularly as measured by economic production. His insights led to a social revolution with deep suspicions of "ideological propaganda" produced by those with capital assets. Marx advocated the use of nearly any means, including violent revolution, to achieve greater equality among the world's "haves" and "have nots."

Theologians and sociologists have sought to apply Marx's insights in the church. Particularly in Latin America, emerging "base communities" in the church developed liberation theology, an approach to justice-making with an attendant means of interpreting the biblical text. Liberation hermeneutics values experience over theory, especially the experience of those suffering extreme poverty under unjust regimes. Employing the "hermeneutics of suspicion," liberation theologians call for a re-examination of the biblical texts which have been used to oppress the poor and oppressed.

Proceeding from the premise that "the organization of a society revolves around its means of production," Leonardo Boff (110), contends that "the Church also is conditioned, limited, and oriented by the specific means of production" and that "the means of production determines which religious-ec-clesiastical activities are impossible, undesirable, intolerable, acceptable, necessary, and primary." He (113) asserts that the institutional church lives with the temptation to over-identify with the ruling class: "the Church has often become the legitimizing religious ideology for the imperial social order." He contends that such a stance contradicts the narration of the story of Jesus Christ and the apostles, who identified with the poor and marginalized in society. His insights buttress the arguments regarding the differences between the free church and Constantinianism in Chapter Two above.

Feminist hermeneutics, often considered a branch of liberation hermeneutics, also exercises the hermeneutics of suspicion, looking for new meanings in old texts, or asking hard questions of the text. In particular, feminists are alert to cases of patriarchal ideology as manifested in either the production or translation of the biblical text. For example, feminists may ask why the apostle Paul did not mention any women in his account of those who saw the risen Christ (1 Cor. 15:5-8) when the Gospels name women as the first witnesses (Matt. 28, Mark 16, Luke 24, and John 20).

Megan McKenna retells Bible stories that are often neglected or undervalued because the experience of women in them is commonly downplayed. Her title, *Not Counting Women and Children*, uses the biblical phrase from Matthew 14:21 as a rubric that demonstrates the frequent neglect or willful submergence of the experience of women, both in ancient and modern life. In a powerful reversal of traditional interpretations of the stories in Genesis, she argues convincingly that Hagar was a woman of strong faith, not to be considered less faithful than Sarah who is the classic "mother in faith."

Further, McKenna argues that Sarah was part of the system that oppressed Hagar as a slave woman. Extending her analysis to the present day, McKenna (185) makes the point that "poor women do theology differently from well-educated, comfortable, and wealthy women of a culture that dominates the cultures of minorities" (in actuality the majority). For the poor around the world, gender is not the main issue, but rather "redistribution of land, housing, education, health care, and responses to violence and abuse" (187).

She continues,

> The reading of the Scriptures by the poor and their inter-
> pretations may make us "disassemble" and confront our
> own biases, call us to account for our own lives in very per-
> sonal responses to injustice and individual people, and
> convict us of insensitivity to others, callousness in our own
> endeavors, and attitudes of racism, selfishness, and self-
> righteousness. (187)

Although they take exception to radical feminist interpretation, Klein et. al. (456) suggest that

> all Bible students, particularly those from more conserva-
> tive backgrounds, would do well to reread Scripture
> through the windows of various feminist perspectives.
> They must be open to see if they have read texts in light of
> their own prevailing, patriarchal cultural biases.

Harder (1998, 20) argues that "radical change and innova-
tion may be needed in the community's theological formulations" when a particular biblical interpretation is deeply in-
grained in a community tradition. A critical strategy "enters the
discourse of a community as a disruption and seeks to transform the language of tradition to resolve the contradictions and
anomalies that have developed in community experience."

She maintains, however, that this strategy, must be held in
tension with a constructive model which "examines how certain convictions, experiences, and texts have shaped the identity and practice of a community" (20). In her mind, a theological method can helpfully incorporate both construction and critique: she "refuses to accept the polarity commonly assumed
by many scholars—a polarity that places commitment and suspicion at opposite ends of objective scholarship" (21). Her assertion suggests a way in which modern scholars may fruitfully
join the hermeneutic community for discernment in modern
times.

The Rhetorical Turn in Hermeneutics

Anabaptist scholars are increasingly aware that one cannot
simply observe behavior; it must be observed through some
kind of terminology. Because of the representative nature of language, any given terminology is both a reflection and a deflec-

tion of reality. Any system of thought necessarily frames, selects, and orders reality in particularized, oversimplified ways. In essence, one's chosen terminology is a terministic screen, a filter through which one views the world. The terminology necessarily directs attention in a certain direction. Modern rhetorical scholars are particularly alert to the ways that particular terminology and the resources of language are used to move others to action or change of attitude or belief. This is the province of rhetorical studies.[17]

Although there are pejorative as well as eulogistic concepts of rhetoric, a relatively *neutral*, pragmatic conception of rhetoric is assumed here. Rhetoric is the form that discourse takes when it goes public; that is, when it has been geared to an audience, readied for an occasion, and adapted to particular ends. Rhetoric is *symbolic inducement—persuasive communication devised to move others to some action or change of attitude*. Therefore, to rhetorically analyze a discourse implies neither censure nor endorsement of the message. Rather, it denotes an assessment of its persuasive power (cf. Warner).

Contemporary and postmodernist rhetorical scholars tend to eschew the modernist, objectivist stance that holds the natural, the observable, to be "real," apart from the problems of language. Rather, rhetorical analysis seeks to lend understanding to the relationship between language and what is observable. Rhetorical scholars study the ways that communities employ language to achieve their ends, relying on various modes of persuasion to promote their ideology and world view. Even scholarly modes of inquiry such as theology, historiography, and biblical hermeneutics depend on rhetoric for persuasive effect.

Patrick and Scult (104) allege that the Bible itself was written for rhetorical effect: "The words of the Bible were written to persuade its audience to right action . . . so it is the success of the text as persuasive discourse which is most likely to account for the power of these stories to endure through time." Again, "the Bible assumes the narrative shape that it does, not because it is the most beautiful or most truthful, but rather because this is the form that is the most persuasive."

Persuasive appeal implies choice; where there is no choice, there can be no inducement, no persuasion. The rhetorical analyst examines the ways that biblical language is used to induce others to make particular choices. Herein lies an important intersection of rhetoric and hermeneutics. The Gospel writer declared: "these [accounts] are written that you may believe that Jesus is the Christ, the Son of God, and that by believing you may have life in his name" (John 20:31). The rhetorical scholar has interest, then, in examining the nature of John's persuasive arguments.

For the most part, modern theologians have not perceived of rhetoric as a resource for Bible study or preaching.[18] But biblical scholars are now exploring the resources of rhetorical analysis for interpreting biblical texts. Phyllis Trible, for example, employs rhetorical analysis to explicate the book of Jonah. As a homiletician, Paul Scott Wilson (65) contends that the discipline of hermeneutics "originates from rhetoric's concern with the purpose of discourse, the form it takes, a consideration of what is persuasive, and understandings of how persuasion happens." In Wilson's (69) mind, the rhetorical gap between the typical insights of systematic theology and the exigencies of the preacher is "a fissure, deep and wide." He (70) asserts that "the sermon is not the dilution, popularization, or translation of theology. It is rather the completion of theology, and is made complete through Christ speaking and constituting the church through it."

Wilson's assertions point to the rhetorical turn in both homiletics and hermeneutics. Rhetoric serves as a link between the biblical text and the exigencies that eventuate in a sermon or teaching in a congregational setting. Hyde and Smith (363) argue that "all interpretation in a sense is rhetorical; all hermeneutics is rhetorical."[19]

Further, they suggest that rhetoric's relationship to hermeneutics is epistemological. The *making known* of a text involves rhetorical strategy—consideration of audience situation and consciousness. The exigencies of the present situation require the rhetor to link the past and the present. Rhetoric draws upon the *historical happening* surrounding a text to enlighten current understanding. At the same time, rhetoric may expand the meaning of a past text into possibilities for meaning in the present. Thus, some of yesterday's "rhetorical visions" have become today's social realities (Hyde and Smith, 356).

Scult argues that the interpretation of Scripture provides a classical exemplar of the hermeneutical enterprise and the relationship between rhetoric and hermeneutics. Several quotations will serve to explicate his understanding of this relationship:

> The impulse to interpret a sacred text is rhetorical. The interpreter sees the text, properly interpreted, as a fitting response to an exigence, something that needs doing, in the rhetorical situation of the interpreter's audience. In this formulation *interpretation is a species of rhetorical invention chosen by the rhetorician-interpreter when there is warrant to extend in time and space the meaning of a sacred text.*
>
> The events and experiences described in the text might remain within the bounds of a spatial-temporal moment, but their meaning reaches beyond that moment. It becomes the task (even the obligation one might say) of the interpreter to enable the text to speak to future audiences—audiences that are just as significant to the meaning of the text as was the "original audience." The rhetorical situation as perceived by the interpreter calls out for a response from the text. *Interpretation becomes the inventional means through which the text is transformed into a fitting response.* The interpretation is thus rhetorically motivated and directed.
>
> After direct revelation ceased, interpretation continues to perform the function that revelation served. This function is a rhetorical one whereby the interpreter enables the text (and the god behind it) to continue to show the way by responding to ever new rhetorical situations. (223-25)

Scult maintains that an emphasis on the meaning of the text in its original setting may tend to suppress its current authority and application. The more adequate the explanation of the original rhetorical exigency that gave rise to the text, the more circumscribed its epistemological range becomes (225). Thus one might expect that the study of the original biblical languages and a survey of biblical history could tend to mute the revelatory and direct authoritative nature of particular texts. In the same way, categorizing biblical materials according to genre may suppress its revelatory feel.

Scult's explication of the relationship between rhetoric and the interpretation of sacred texts is particularly apt for a critical understanding of biblical *prophecy*, where there is a good deal of ambiguity regarding the time period when predicted events are (or were) to take place. When an adequate historical explanation can be given to demonstrate that the prophetic text has been *fulfilled*, the meaning and power of the text for the current situation is greatly reduced.

Patrick and Scult (1990) attempt to refine a new rhetorical methodology which takes into account critical historical analysis as well as the rhetorical exigencies of the text. They posit that the meaning of the text grows out of a rhetorical transaction: "The text is meaningful only to someone who seeks to understand it as an engaged 'subject'" (20). This contrasts with the historical-critical tendency to see the text as object. This does not displace the need for an historical perspective. Rather, it attempts to "judge which moments in a text's history constitute the effective movements of meaning from the text to the interpreter" (20).

Patrick and Scult (22) also acknowledge the importance of the hermeneutical community. They assert that "rhetorical re-enactment of the text's meaning takes place within an interpretive community—a religious community and/or a community of scholars. This community has passed on the knowledge necessary for interpretation and the framework in which it expects the knowledge to be understood."

Further, they assert that the exegete's work can aim to convince the community that the proposed exegesis is the best reading. The community, however, "can judge whether this interpretation and the reasoning supporting it in fact do so according to its standards for making such judgments" (23). Their comments lead naturally to a discussion of contemporary concepts of hermeneutic community.

Contemporary Concepts of Hermeneutic Community

In keeping with their Anabaptist roots, contemporary free church communities have embraced the concept of the church as a hermeneutic community. Before its merger to help form Mennonite Church USA, the General Conference Mennonite Church (*A Christian Declaration*, 19) declared,

The meaning of the Bible cannot be truly apprehended except as mediated through the living and believing fellowship of the Spirit. . . . Each book must be interpreted within the fellowship of believers in accord with the light given to the church by the Spirit in a given time or situation.

Another denomination put it in shorter words: "The Bible is to be interpreted within the context of the believing, obedient community, as that community seeks to communicate its message to the world." (*Biblical Interpretation*, 248)

A biblical base for these assertions are found in what is sometimes called "the rule of Paul." In his instructions to the Corinthian church, the apostle outlined a process by which prophets would speak and the congregation weigh what was said (1 Cor. 14:29). For John Driver (1976, 15-17), this means that "the gathered congregation, rather than its authorities, theologians, and prophets, is responsible for discerning the will of God. In the exercise of his hermeneutic prerogative the common ordinary Christian acts as a full member of the body of Christ." In the true hermeneutic community, no one individual is solely responsible for declaring God's word. The group's participation provides both a protection from individualism and the abuse of authority. Further, the combined gifts and perspectives of various individuals will bring fuller understanding to the interpretive task (Yoder, 1982, 51).

It is the community of faith that brings the authority of the Bible to bear in modern life. As John Howard Yoder (1994, 353) contends: "the most complete framework in which to affirm the authority of Scripture is the context of its being read and applied by a believing people that uses its guidance to respond to concrete issues in their witness and obedience."

Marlin Miller (K and K, 42) expresses a similar opinion: "The church as the community of the new covenant of grace constitutes the primary locus of moral discernment and accountability for the Christian." Kniss (35) echoes the same belief: "The Bible in and of itself can hardly be understood to be authoritative in any practical way, apart from its engagement with a community of faith that acknowledges its authority for them." He contends that only in accountability to a faith community will individuals truly live in submission to biblical authority.

It is the hermeneutic community, then, that becomes a primary place of encounter between the written word of Scripture and the contemporary world. As Harder (1984, 45) asserts,

> it has never been enough to only receive and transmit an authoritative word from the past. The recognition that God is not only a God of the past, but also of the present and future has meant that interpretation is not a static event, but rather a dynamic open-ended process.

In a similar vein, Lind (1984, 155) observes that the church looks for analogies to gain understanding of today's events in the light of biblical revelation. Citing Millard Lind, Miller (K and K 216) asserts that "it is only within the life situation of the hermeneutical community that the fundamental analogies are experienced which make the Bible historically credible."

> The church today, as an historical reality and directed by the Holy Spirit becomes the place of analogy with the New Testament church, rather than the contemporary world being seen as the place of analogy with the ancient world at the time of the New Testament.

The interpretation of Scripture is not esoteric and theoretical but public and particular both in focus and application. Harder (1984, 26-7) asserts that "for Anabaptists and Mennonites the goal of the hermeneutical process can be described as being contemporary, concrete, and particular. It can be expressed as discernment leading to obedience, particularly in the areas of morality and ethics." Further, she (1984, 118) suggests that from the perspective of action-reflection, "it is the concrete pastoral situation of the Christian community which must determine not only the questions asked of Scripture, but also in some sense the shape of biblical interpretation and proclamation."

Swartley (1983, 216f.) believes the concept of hermeneutic community has several implications for the way Scripture is viewed in the life of the church. For one, the contemporary interpreter must pay attention to the horizontal axis of communication between divine initiative and resulting faith communities, the encounter which first produced and now discloses the Scriptures. There is a "movement from earlier to later testimony, especially because Scripture dialogues with and critiques itself." Schroeder (1987) too suggests that the community must pay attention to the diversity of experience reflected in many stages in the production of the biblical text, from the writing to transmission.

Secondly, Swartley (1984, 216) contends, the study of biblical origins has implications for the debate over the relative primacy of biblical authority vis-a-vis the church community. The historical origins of the Bible lie in communities of faith; those people gave the later church the Bible. The interpretive process must recognize the inseparable relationship between the Bible and the church that produced it. The existence of both may be credited to the creative work of God's Spirit. The same Spirit that produced the text out of the life of a ancient community of faith will enable the contemporary community to interpret it faithfully.

Finally, it is only in such communities of faith, Swartley (1983, 217) contends, that "the credibility and applicability" of the Bible's claims are appropriately tested. "And only within such communities should one expect to find the spiritual resources essential to the motivation and empowerment for living as the biblical teachings envision."

Contemporary scholars have not only endorsed the concept of hermeneutical community but have also discussed its particular limitations. Not only individuals, but also groups, can be limited by their traditions and ideological perspectives. Harder (1984, 155) contends that "tradition comes to us as a mixed stream of human sinfulness as well as God's grace. Rituals and language forms can become dead and ideological. The critique of the prophet is needed to help open the traditions to new life."

Harder (1984, 76) draws on philosophical theory to demonstrate the importance of pre-understanding—the traditions, institutional habits, and modes of discourse which faith communities bring to their understanding of Scripture. She argues that the historical mediators of Scripture, be they persons, institutions, or methodologies, may hinder genuine understanding of the text. Power relationships, for example, may create systemic distortion.

She maintains that as the hermeneutic community practices critical reflection, it engages in "a dialectical process between the prophetic voice and the consensus of tradition" (Harder 1984, 158).

As a woman, Harder is particularly alert to the ways that communities of faith have excluded or undervalued the witness of women. In her mind, the feminist concern for salvation and liberation for all persons "presents a particular challenge to Mennonites to spell out more clearly the shape of the hermeneutic community. As the definition of salvation is enlarged and adjusted to include the experience of women, the particular limitations and strengths of a specific hermeneutic community will be evident" (47). As women share experiences of liberation with their faith communities, she contends, "communal traditions, communal structures and institutions, and communal language will be challenged by their insights and critiques" (Harder, 1987, 53).

Citing the work of Schüssler Fiorenza, Harder (1994, 133) articulates the need for hermeneutic communities to name their "political allegiances and presuppositions, " including "a certain androcentric grasp of reality." These are the ideologies which are unearthed by the hermeneutics of suspicion. Yet, as Harder herself maintains: "not every ideology implicit in a given historical praxis is necessarily negative or must be qualified. For ideology is also the instrument through which Christian obedience gains coherence and unity" (129).

The exclusiveness or provincialism of the local church may at times serve to limit the effectiveness of the local church (or even the institutional church) as a hermeneutic community. This may force marginalized persons, as Harder (1984, 146) contends, to "recognize God's kingdom outside the borders of the institutional church." In her mind, the hermeneutical community extends beyond the institutional church to

> any group which shares the vision of the people of God as the discipleship of equals, and dares to live according to this vision in its concrete social situation. In the obedient community, the relationships between persons will reflect mutual respect and recognition, rather than hierarchical power struggles. Only in such a dialogical community will authoritative truth emerge.

This dialogue includes the church as a hermeneutic community on different levels, as Yoder (1994, 352) contends: "The Bible uses the term church for all of the Christians in a large city or even in a province." Therefore, while the local church provides the practical and theological foundation for discernment, it is not the only legitimate form of church. "There are mutual responsibilities between Christians of different congregations." Dialogue with Christians in other church communities may alert us to our pre-understandings and unexamined commitments. Nevertheless, Harder (1994, 29) insists that "the testing and application of an interpretation begins in a small setting, and only then moves to larger groups and associations of congregations, not vice versa."

Sometimes biblical scholars will find themselves in tension "between their loyalties to the scholarly community with its scientific methodological approaches, and their commitments to the church community in its dogmatic and preaching tradition" (Harder 1984, 104). Harder contends that this tension is not necessarily negative, observing that churches can sometimes benefit from greater openness to the social and political arena in their discernment process. Whereas they have typically drawn tight boundaries between church and world, they could helpfully recognize that God acts even through those "who do not explicitly recognize Christian faith" (Harder 1984, 151). She believes that

> Dialogue and interaction with those outside the church boundaries is basic to the hermeneutical process. For contemporary practical theology the hermeneutic community is therefore located not so much in the gathered institutional church, but in the scattered church active in mission in the world. (Harder, 1984, 151)

In this context, the movement from "Word to life" takes place most authentically.

SUMMARY

This chapter has attempted to capture the essence of sixteenth-century Anabaptist hermeneutics, both as expressed in broad principles and more specifically in regard to the discerning hermeneutic community. In addition to the disclaimers about the authenticity of the popular tradition, we have observed some scholarly reservations about traditional Anabaptist hermeneutic practices. In addition, we have expounded on the significant shift between sixteenth-century Anabaptist practice and contemporary application, due at least partly to the effects of modernization on the church.

Nevertheless, modern Anabaptists at least theoretically uphold the value of the hermeneutic community as the best place to interpret the Bible. The next chapter examines some of the dialectical and practical tensions that such communities face as they seek to discern God's will for the contemporary Christian life.

NOTES

1. Cf. a series of articles in Swartley (1984) Part I, under the heading "Interpretation of Anabaptist Sources." Snyder (159) suggests that there were three phases in the development of Anabaptist hermeneutics. The first stage "defined" the movement as Anabaptist by agreement on "the meaning and centrality of a core of biblical texts relating to church reform." The second stage saw the development of a movement "in spite of" significant hermeneutical differences as "Anabaptists worked out concrete implications based upon their common core of biblical texts and principles." The third stage brought a "narrower consensus on an interpretive approach."

2. In Stutzman (1993), I discuss at some length the effect of secularization on modern consciousness, with the attendant effect on nonresistance, one of the central doctrines of the Mennonite Church.

3. Modern social science theory has assumed that religious societies, along with other forms of particularity, would give way to the integrative pressures of modernization, urbanization, and global economic systems. Certainly, Mennonite beliefs have been very much affected by the Mennonite experience of secularization in the American context. Nevertheless, it may be said that the Mennonite story exemplifies the enduring character of communal and convictional religious groupings in the face of modern pressures to conform. Toews (1989, 245) suggested that "the straight-line logic of modernization theory failed to take into account the persistence and social inventiveness of communities with their own sense of particularity and their ability to preserve and even extend themselves." The grand paradigm of understanding Western history as an inevitable move away from religion is increasingly under assault.

4. The experience of conservatism in its encounter with modernity is

not paradigmatic for all orthodoxies—Catholicism, Orthodox Judaism, Islam, and Buddhism. This is partially true because orthodoxy is defined so differently for various faiths: for Catholics, it is loyalty to the church; for Orthodox Jews, it is commitment to the Torah and the community that supports it; for Islam, it is behavioral conformity to Sharia; and for Buddhism, it is defined mainly in devotional terms, if at all (Hunter 1987 238). Because Mennonites have emphasized *orthopraxy* as opposed to *orthodoxy*, they have as a denomination responded with less intensity to the secular threat than have other evangelical groups, such as the Southern Baptists (See Ammerman).

5. One of the most important changes that has taken place in the broader American religious scene is the decline in tension between Catholics and Protestants, between Christians and Jews, and between different Protestant denominations (Wuthnow, 1989, *Struggle*, 15). Intermarriage, ecumenical activities, and generally increased tolerance has brought new levels of social interaction among religious groups. The old system broke up gradually, aided by social activism, war protest, and dissension on college campuses. The tripartite system of religion in America (Protestant, Catholic, Jew) suggested by Herberg (1960) has come to be replaced by a two-part system (Cf. Wuthnow, 1988).

6. Cf. Lindsell's *Battle for the Bible*.

7. Cf. Zoba, who describes the forty-year process of translating the New Testament for a small tribe in the jungles of Peru. Using the principles of translation taught by the Summer Institute of Linguistics, the missionaries "aim to preserve the meaning of the original text in a way that is understood in the community according to their customs and language structures" (23). Using the mutual cognitive environment, they drew on the metaphor of freshly peeled yucca to express the whiteness, describing both the cleansing that comes from sin and the appearance of Jesus on the Mount of Transfiguration (Isa. 1:18, Matt. 17:2). The receptor tribe, the Sharanahua, do not leave father and mother when they marry; they live in the same house. Thus, the missionaries expressed the concept of "leaving and cleaving" (Matt.19:5) with the expression: "For this reason a man shall have the same mosquito net as his wife." This was the cultural equivalent.

8. Cf. Thomas (1) for a critical scrutiny of the theory behind dynamic equivalence and a comparison with older theories of biblical translation.

9. Grudem and Osborne took two different sides in the debate, both admitting there are serious challenges to translation for modern day readers.

10. Among the new inclusive-language texts are the *Contemporary English Version*, the *New Revised Standard Version*, the *New Living Translation*, *God's Word*, *the New Century Version*, and the *New International*

Version (Inclusive Language Edition). Because of strong protest from conservative opponents, the latter was pulled off the market in the United States.

11. The ordinance of the Holy Kiss has been taught in the Amish and Mennonite expressions of the free church up to modern times. Brunk cited the scriptures which enjoined the holy kiss as a religious duty, arguing that it "nourishes and gives emphatic expression to the greatest and most indispensable principle of the Christian religion, that of spiritual love" (83).

12. 1 Corinthians 16:20 is variously translated: "Give each other a warm greeting," "Pass the greetings around with holy embraces," and "Give each other a loving handshake when you meet" in respective order, by the *Contemporary English Version, The Message,* and the *Living New Testament.*

13. Much of my wording in this paragraph and in this section through discussion of CPS, VS, and I-W service on p. 74 draws on my dissertation, Stutzman (1993, 60-64). Wuthnow (1989, *Communities,* 540) stated:

> To understand how an ideology is shaped by its social environment, one must therefore examine the specific circumstances under which these expressions came into being, the audience to whom they are enunciated, the slogans and other materials that are available at the time for incorporation into discursive acts, the roles of speakers and audiences relative to one another and in relation to positions of power, and even the financial resources that make publishing activities possible. Examining these contexts of ideological production enables one to establish with greater clarity whey a particular constellation of ideas comes to be institutionalized successfully in a particular setting.

15. Recasting Berger's conceptualization somewhat, Simons, Mechling, and Schreier (812) explained the dialectical, interactive relationship among *"situation* (both as 'external force' and as rhetorical creation), *audience* (both as cultural or societal 'out there' and as a rhetor's particular audience), and *rhetor* (both as actor and as reactor)."

16. Redekop argues that sect groups, such as the Anabaptists, have resisted the seduction of culture by resisting total ideology. Thus, they have taken different stances than the state on issues of war, wealth and poverty, domination, ethnocentrism, and nationalism. Resisting the Constantinian state, they have sought to live in communities of faith, committed to following Jesus. He believes that the Anabaptists were protected from the effects of total ideology by two practices: (1) living under the rule of the scriptures as a transcendent source of knowledge, rather than above the scriptures by "interpreting" them as did the other Reformers, and (2) applying the insights from that transcendent source of knowledge "through the crucible of the nurture and admonition of the group." "Since they were aware of the individual source of distor-

tion and deception, their interpretation of something as holy as the transcendent source of knowledge could not be left to individual whims, but had to be entrusted to the reasoned and balanced insights of the group in a collective search" (103).

17. The deliberate use and study of rhetoric has had an uneasy alliance with the Christian church from its founding. In his letter to the Corinthians, The Apostle Paul poignantly denied the use of persuasive speech. His declaration was perhaps prompted by the memory of his speech in the city of Athens, the seedbed of Greek rhetoric. In the address at the Areopagus, Paul made no reference to Jesus Christ or the crucifixion of Christ (Acts 17:22-31). To the Corinthians (2:2) he declared that from then on, he would only preach Christ, and him crucified. Nevertheless, the apostle wrote letters to the churches with urgency and persuasive appeal. And he consciously spoke of the importance of persuasion.

Several centuries later, Saint Augustine wrote about rhetoric in his spiritual biography, the *Confessions*. A teacher of pagan rhetoric who confessed to having lived a perverted life until his conversion to Christianity, Augustine contended that the resources of rhetorical persuasion could benefit the Christian religion. Burke found rich resources in Augustine's writings to demonstrate the use of persuasion in the formulation of Christian doctrine, particularly through language about the Trinity.

18. Nevertheless, Litfin (14) argues that some contemporary preachers depend more upon the insights of rhetoric than they do upon the example of the apostolic preachers. He asserts that in Broadus' classic homiletics text, *On the Preparation and Delivery of Sermons*, the discussion on how to construct and deliver sermons is more indebted to Aristotle and Cicero than it is to the practice of Peter and Paul. He worries that modern preachers, employing the means of persuasion, might falsely "convert" persons to Christianity, winning them into the fellowship of the church without a genuine spiritual change.

19. Much of my wording citing the works of Hyde and Smith, Scult, and Patrick and Scult on pp. 78-80 draws on Stutzman (1993, 271-273).

CHAPTER 4

·····················

WORKING WITH DIFFER-ENCES IN COMMUNAL DISCERNMENT PROCESSES

CHURCH GROUPS TYPICALLY ESCHEW DIFFERENCES, bidding instead for peace and quiet. Nevertheless, amid discernment about the will of God, congregations generally face a variety of differences—ideological, theological, biblical, and practical. The various ideas which are propounded in communal discussions, all based on Scripture and orthodox theology, may introduce paradox, dilemmas, and interdependent opposites. The differing gifts, interests, and perspectives that people contribute to the discernment processes may sometime result in relatively high levels of interpersonal conflict. In fact, close-knit groups have far more potential for conflict than those with members who are distant from each other.

Further, when the issues being discussed relate to deeply held values and group members care passionately about outcomes, potential for conflict is especially high. Therefore, this study assumes that a certain amount of tension due to differences may be viewed as normal and healthy components of the discernment process. Differences or tensions may be expressed in various ways. This chapter explores creative ways to deal with these differences in a discerning hermeneutic community.

A DIALECTICAL APPROACH
TO IDEOLOGICAL TENSIONS

One of the marks of a creative mind is the ability to think paradoxically. As Scott Fitzgerald has said, "The test of a first-rate intelligence is the ability to hold two opposed ideas in mind at the same time and still retain the ability to function" (quoted in Johnson 55). Blaise Pascal said: "A person does not prove his or her greatness by standing at an extremity, but by touching both extremities at once and filling all that lies between them" (quoted in Jacobsen, 441). Leonard Sweet maintains that "a key to doing ministry in postmodern culture[1] is understanding this one thing: Opposite things happen at the same time and they aren't contradictory."

Perhaps in group discernment more than any other time, wise people need to look beyond traditional extremities to find an integrative way to work. Life in any community does not remain tranquil or well-ordered for long. Sooner or later, values will clash.

As Rokeach has shown, individuals and ideologies "can be systematically distinguished by the relative weight placed upon a small number of values." For example, "there is evidence to show that conservatives and liberals differ in their readiness to blame the poor or the inequalities of society for the existence of poverty" (in Billig, 215). The most deeply held values show up in the proverbs or maxims of a people, passing on ideas like genetic material to the next generation. The Proverbs of the Old Testament reflect the deeply held values of the Israelite people. Yet these values in those proverbs, like the ones today, often come into conflict in everyday life. In modern America, the following two maxims may vie for hegemony: "Many hands make work light" and "Too many cooks spoil the broth." In any given situation, one must decide (perhaps quickly) which of the values to embrace for the particular moment.

A pair of proverbs that are likely to "tussle" with one another are found in Proverbs 26:4-5. The counsel: "Do not answer a fool according to his folly, or you will be like him yourself," is followed by the contrary counsel: "Answer a fool according to his folly, or he will be wise in his own eyes." This counsel reflects the reality of everyday life—when you're dealing with a fool, anything you say can get you in trouble. In this vein, Michael Billig argues that "following Quintillian's Principle of Uncertainty, we can say that there is an infinity of situations or conditions in which contrary proverbs may be applicable" (212).

Pareto argues that following any one principle to its ultimate conclusion (to the exclusion of counter-principles) would spell social disaster. Therefore, he contends that each principle based on values must be balanced by other principles. In Billig's words, "for most social actions, there will be a complexity of principles pushing and tugging in different directions." "In each case, an eminently sensible principle is hauled back by an equally sensible counter-principle." The social dilemmas that arise as a result of trying to apply principles based on values are not "'unfortunate accidents' but rather the inevitable consequence of there being principles or values" (212). Even a hierarchy of values will not solve all of the dilemmas. There seems to be no way to escape from the need for continual discernment to sort through the dilemmas of everyday life.

Klyne Snodgrass (32) asserts that tensions are an indispensable part of the framework for Christian living,[2] like the taut strings on a finely tuned instrument. "If a string is left loose, music cannot be produced. If it is stretched too tight, the string will break" (32). He offers several guidelines for living with tensions in the church. "The first guideline is to practice holistic thinking," which in humility recognizes that "no single statement can be identified with the whole truth" (183). Holistic thinking recognizes tensions both in the modern world and between biblical texts. He asserts that biblical writers dealt with tensions just as we do.[3]

Second, Snodgrass suggests that a way to handle a good deal of tension is to "allow for unity and diversity within the church" (185). Rejecting the idea of Aristotle's "golden mean," Snodgrass asserts,

> Christians have the responsibility of holding both extremes and the middle in their hands and then of choosing how the tensions may be lived justly in each situation. The grace of God, which provides the coherence to our lives, is the power by which we live out our tensions. We live between truths. (191).

Swartley (1983) maintains that there is both unity and diversity of thought found in the Scriptures. There are tensions between ideas propounded in various texts, not only between the two testaments, but within the New Testament itself. Interpretive approaches to these texts differ radically depending on one's view of Scripture and one's own ideology.[4] For Swartley, "coherence amid the diversity is expected not at the level where all statements say the same thing, or where all expressions of faith are uniform, but rather at the point of seeking fidelity to the central testimony" (232).[5]

Throughout the history of the church, the church has swung back and forth between different emphases like a pendulum. Robert Walton has diagramed this tendency in regard to primary emphasis on emotions vs. intellect, showing how various movements[6] have drawn the church in either one direction or the other. He contends that biblical Christianity is found somewhere between the poles (78).

In response to the debate regarding Anabaptist historiography, Sawatsky also appeals for a dialectical approach, which "might well hold a variety of positions in tension; optimism and pessimism about outside influences, theological ideals and historical realities, perfection and sin, restitutionism and development, Mennonite particularism and Christian ecumenism, etc." (20). He maintains that a dialectical approach "learns from its Anabaptist past as it formulates a Mennonite theology in conversation with other Christian traditions in the common pursuit of faithfulness to Christ in the present and the future" (20). This study assumes the value of a dialectical approach, positing that truth is ultimately found that way.

The Value of a Dialectical Approach

Particularly in a postmodern environment, it is helpful to examine issues from various perspectives or points of view.[7] One need not accept Marxist materialism or Hegelian philosophy[8] to appreciate the value of examining opposing points of view. A dialectical approach simply examines the two (or more) sides of an argument to come to the truth. In some of the examples below, I use the rubric of "idea pairs" to indicate the two "poles" or "sides" of an issue that are expressed in a matched pair of terms such as "law vs. grace." Each of the terms in these idea pairs gains much of its meaning in contrast (or interaction) with the other. Working creatively with linguistic tensions in a dialectic approach has the potential to contribute significantly to the communal discernment process.

In fact, failure to consider seriously the tensions introduced by various perspectives can lead to unbalanced Christian living, incomplete theology, or even serious heresy. This is quickly made evident by a couple of examples of major doctrines, derived from Scripture, which hold truths in tension with one another. For example, one aspect of Christological doctrine may be seen as a tension between the divinity and the humanity of Jesus Christ. Emphasizing Christ's divinity to the neglect of Christ's humanity leads to the heresy of Docetism. Emphasizing Christ's humanity to the neglect of Christ's divinity leads to Arianism.

Similarly, theologians posit a tension between the transcendence and immanence of God. Emphasis on one pole of the idea pair with the corresponding neglect of the other leads to heresies such as Deism and Pantheism. Many other "idea pairs," with corresponding heresies, could be explicated in similar manner.[9] Throughout church history, heated debates around particular theological "idea pairs" have led to doctrinal formulations and creeds. One such idea pair debated in some faith communities is "complementarity[10] vs. equality" as a description of the biblical role relationship of women and men in the community of faith.

Theological/Biblical Tensions in Anabaptist Perspective

While every Christian community deals with biblical tensions, some tensions are particularly salient to particular communities at particular times. Church communions often develop a "canon within a canon" and a particular system of theology to help bring coherence to their understanding and expression of Christian life. As a result, communities distinguish themselves by their placement on the theological and practical continuum of various idea pairs.

This is a seemingly natural result of the discerning process. One can learn much about the nature of a community by examining the idea pairs which it emphasizes. A number of idea pairs stand out in the literature on free church ecclesiology. The purpose here is to provide a brief survey of these idea pairs, with relatively brief explanation. There is no attempt to be exhaustive. Some idea pairs are primarily theological, forming the doctrinal foundation for the church. Others are more practical, dealing with the hermeneutical process in the community.

Church vs. world

The church vs. world idea pair was a common (and sharply drawn) dichotomy in sixteenth century Anabaptism, closely related to the dualism of the two kingdoms. Discussions about the nature of the church[11], particularly in the Dutch context, reflected the sincere desire to keep the church pure, separate from the world. Krahn (1958) observes: "Particularly did the Dutch Anabaptists emphasize Paul's teaching about the church being the bride or the body of Christ and the temple of God which was to be blameless and without spot or wrinkle" (64). "Scripture passages which are quoted again and again are Ephesians 5:25, 27, 30; 1 Corinthians 12:25-27; 2 Corinthians 6:14." This desire was the motivating force behind church discipline.

The idea of church discipline, of course, was not new. Klaassen (1981, 211) asserts that what we call persecution today was viewed by sixteenth-century Catholics and Protestants as church discipline, often involving "imprisonment, torture, exile, deprivation of property, and even death." Anabaptists, however, tried to follow the "rule of Christ." Since Anabaptists saw a clear distinction between the church and the world, they excommunicated unrepentant members by sending them into the world, the kingdom of Satan (Krahn, 1981, 211).

Anabaptists rejected torture, imprisonment, and death as appropriate means of discipline. For them, the Ban was their only "sword" (Littell, 67). "In some cases experiencing the Ban might mean social ostracism (shunning, *Meidung*), but generally it meant the loss of privileges within the brotherhood" (Littell, 86). "Many offenses resulted only in temporary exclusion from fellowship of the Lord's Supper (called the small ban), but in dire cases, members could be excommunicated (the big ban) although even then reconciliation was possible and, in fact, the ideal" (Sprunger, 204).

In the first part of this century, Mennonites articulated their unique Christian identity primarily through the rubrics of nonconformity and nonresistance, the "Siamese twins"[12] of Mennonite identity. These two deep-seated values served to keep the church separate from the world. In contemporary Anabaptism, however, "world" is seen not so much as the domain of the prince of darkness (as it was in early Anabaptism), but more as the secular realm of life apart from the institutional church. Some Anabaptist scholars, for example, express themselves in contrast to the Niebuhrian project that seeks ways to transform culture through participation in the world. Redekop believes that the concept of relevance to culture itself reveals a cultural bias. Like Driver he asserts that the church must be a *contrast* society.

At the same time, Anabaptist scholars have worked at ways for the church to address the problems of society.[13] Beginning in the late 1950s, some scholars (see Concern Movement below) worked at ways for Christians to exercise social responsibility in the world. They developed the concept of "middle axioms" to bridge the value gap between the church and the world.[14] Ultimately these ideas practically displaced the earlier concepts of nonconformity and nonresistance, with their negative sense of disengagement with the world.

The idea pair of church vs. world has clear implications for the hermeneutic community. Communities with a sectarian vision read the Bible as though they were God's "peculiar" people, sanctified by God's grace. This impulse to holiness inevitably leads to discussions about who is in and who is out of the church body. Voolstra (20) observes that "the pursuit of holiness is always at odds with the preservation of unity, whether of church and society or of the church itself. Anabaptism is a good illustration of this pattern in church history."

According to Krahn (1958, 67), "the greatest differences [in the Dutch church] arose in connection with the demarcation lines between the true church and the world, between the things permissible for a Christian and those not permissible."

In the end, the elders' zeal to establish a pure church without spot or wrinkle led to infamous factions in the Dutch church. Today, descendants of the Anabaptism have a variety of practice regarding church discipline and excommunication. Some regularly use the ban, while others exercise little or no recognizable church discipline.

The discerning hermeneutic community, then, faces the hard question of deciding how to enforce, if at all, the boundary between church and world. In today's American context of individualism and civil rights, inclusiveness is a high value. For the church to excommunicate persons based on differences in values or behavior may readily be interpreted as undue exclusiveness.

Jacobsen argues that perhaps "discernment" (as opposed to "exclusivity"), may best serve as the ideal opposite pole for "inclusivity" in the modern context. "Inclusivity directs us to accept and welcome anyone truly seeking to be a follower of Jesus; discernment emphasizes that Christian discipleship is not a glib undertaking. Inclusivity reminds us of the wonder of God's open-armed grace; discernment reminds us that grace is not cheap" (441). The discerning community will benefit from holding both of these "extremes" in mind as it seeks to be a faithful church amid the world.

Church vs. kingdom

Some of the earliest recorded words of Jesus are a proclamation of the coming kingdom (Matt. 4:17, Mark 1:15). His teaching was filled with references to the kingdom.[15] There are however, only two references in the Gospels to the church (Matt.16:18; 18:15-20). In contrast, the Acts and the epistles have many references to the church, while also mentioning the kingdom. This difference invites reflection on the relationship between the church and the kingdom.

Anabaptist scholars write with deep conviction about this idea pair. Lederach provides a cogent synthesis between church and kingdom:

> Both the church and the kingdom are present realities. God is working through the church today. The church and the kingdom are not separated. However, the church and the kingdom are not identical. The church is not the kingdom, yet the church is inexplicably interwoven with the

kingdom. The church proclaims the good news of the kingdom. The church is entrusted with the kingdom. Jesus said that the church is given the keys of the kingdom. Thus the church opens and closes the gates of the kingdom (Matt. 16:18, 19). The church has a responsibility to maintain the integrity of the fellowship under the rule of God. (33)

Kraus echoes this emphasis: "The kingdom of God is the reality of which the church is a sign. To speak of the church as a sign is to describe it as a kind of evidence (witness)." "Only as an authentic sign can it be a credible witness" (182). Miller (K and K) speaks in similar fashion:

The New Testament does not simply equate the church with the kingdom of God. The kingdom is always greater than the church, even though the life of the Christian community should never be less than a visible manifestation that the reign of God has "come near." (86)

Anabaptist scholars tend to look askance at Fundamentalists such as Darby, believing they unduly separate the church and kingdom through a dispensational view of history.[16] Dispensational theologians see the church as God's agency to save people's souls in preparation for a kingdom that is to come later.[17] This represents a radical discontinuity between the church and the kingdom, relegating the church to a secondary role.[18] It also dismisses too easily the moral and ethical demands of Christ's kingdom teachings as mandates applicable only to a future age.

On the other hand, Anabaptist scholars eschew state churches, believing they unduly join church and kingdom in triumphalism. Post-millennial theologians may view the church as God's present reign on earth, closely aligned with nation-states. This is the primary temptation of Constantinianism. It too quickly identifies God's reign with temporal structures, making it difficult to bring either state or church under the proper critique of the Scriptures.

Recognizing the church as a community of the kingdom, or as a sign or foretaste of the kingdom, holds the concepts of church and kingdom in dynamic tension. The hermeneutic community then stands under the ethical mandates of Christ's teaching regarding the kingdom yet does not identify itself as a human institution with God's transcendent reign.[19]

Kingdom future vs. kingdom present

The concept of the *timing* of the kingdom is integrally related to the idea of church and kingdom, discussed just above. Typically, the kingdom is discussed under the theological rubric of eschatology, the study of the future or the end. Lately, however, eschatology has come to signify more than a doctrine of end times. The concept of eschatology may be extended, however, to describe "the present and future reality of the kingdom of God as the new reality of God's reign which has already come in Jesus Christ and which is the final goal of human history." It also has to do with "a theological understanding of the all embracing goal and purpose of history, of its present as well as its future shape, and of the way in which the goal of history gives meaning to human existence and to all of reality." (Miller in K and K, 83).

Jesus began his preaching mission with the words "the kingdom of heaven is near" (Matt. 4:17). He taught his disciples to pray: "[May] your kingdom come. . ." (Matt. 6:10). He told his disciples that they would "not taste death" before they saw "the Son of man coming in his kingdom" (Matt. 16:28). Therefore, he transferred to his disciples a strong sense of anticipation of the presence of the kingdom.

Thomas Finger, an Anabaptist scholar, wrote a two-volume systematic theology using eschatology as the integrating rubric. Speaking of the early followers of Jesus, he declares (Vol I, 102) that

> the eschatological atmosphere of the "already/not yet" pervades every action and thought. Ultimately it does not matter whether the consummation is near or far off. In either case hope of Christ's return puts all things in a new perspective.

An eschatological perspective brings the hope of the future into the present. It energizes the church and gives perspective on the church's task. Therefore, we can conclude that ecclesiology and eschatology are fruitfully linked to each other.

In this vein, Miller contends that the church is called to acknowledge the "eschatological priority of the reign of God" and become "a transformed and transforming community as the sign and prefiguration of the new age amid, in solidarity with, and for the sake of the world." (K and K, 90).[20] And Yoder boldly asserts that

> The most significant contributions to history have in the past been made . . . by the "sectarians" whose eschatological consciousness made it sensible for them to act in apparently irresponsible ways. The most effective way to contribute to the preservation of a society in the old aeon is to live in the new. (1994, 165)

Yoder contends that "Schweitzer's thesis, generally accepted by liberal theologians, that the eschatological expectancy of the early church led to ethical irresponsibility,[21] is simply wrong, exegetically and historically" (157-8). What one believes about the future makes a significant difference in the way one acts in the present.

Thomas Finger explicates three broad systems of theology that have arisen to provide a framework for interpreting biblical teaching on eschatology—dispensationalism, existentialism, and post-millennialism. Dispensationalists assume a fairly radical discontinuity between the present order and the future, when all things will be brought to a swift and decisive end. Perhaps most importantly for this study, dispensationalism employs hermeneutics that assume a rather literal fulfillment of prophecy, particularly those concerning Israel as a nation.

In contrast, existentialism assumes figurative language, regarding as mythical the New Testament supernatural claims and eschatological worldview. Bultmann proposed a scheme of biblical and theological reinterpretation under the rubric of "demythologization," dismantling the myths and finding only subjective hope in the promise of the coming kingdom. Post-millennialism as an eschatological approach looks for literal fulfillment of end-time prophecies but without pressing the details. It anticipates the presence of the kingdom in the current age, gradually influencing the world through God's reign.

Although there are varieties of postmillennialism, Finger considers it to be the best overall schema for interpreting Scriptures having to do with the end times. Many contemporary Anabaptists, however, have been significantly influenced by Fundamentalism and its accompanying Dispensationalism. While postmillennialists tend to interpret Scriptures on the side of the "already," dispensationalists clearly interpret Scripture on the side of the "not yet." This idea pair will likely remain as an ongoing tension within the Anabaptist tradition.

Discipleship vs. justification

There are a number of idea pairs that relate very closely to the concept of discipleship vs. justification, including judgment vs. grace, obedience vs. belief, conviction vs. compassion, and ethics vs. doctrine. I have chosen the former because these terms perhaps best capture the essence of the debate between Anabaptists and the other Reformers over the nature of Christian responsibility.

H. S. Bender (1971) believes that the concept of discipleship is "the most characteristic, most central, most essential and regulative concept in Anabaptist thought, which largely determines all else." He also believes that discipleship stands at "the parting of the ways between various forms of Christianity, and various types of theology and ethics" (39). He defines the concept by contending that

> to be a disciple meant to teach and to observe all things whatsoever the Master had taught and commanded. This absolute discipleship applied to all areas of life. It meant a church composed only of disciples, not a mixture of disciples and worldlings. (43)

Responding to the major Reformers' theology of justification, Bender (1962) declared that

> it is a faulty Gospel preaching which limits the gospel offer to forgiveness, and does not describe the grace of God as the way of life. Discipleship is not something which can be added afterward as a secondary but nonessential possibility, or as something for advanced Christians. When the gospel is so understood, it is distorted. (100-101)

John Howard Yoder explicated the Anabaptist emphasis on discipleship primarily as a concern for ethics. He defined discipleship as a particular concern for obeying the ethical mandates of Scripture, particularly those of Jesus Christ.[22] Ac-

102 DISCERNING GOD'S WILL TOGETHER

cording to Murray, (265) "Anabaptists saw obedience not only as the goal of hermeneutics, but as a crucial prerequisite of hermeneutics" (265). He saw it as the main point of Hans Denck's oft-quoted saying that "No one can know Christ unless he follows after him in life, and no one can follow him unless he first know him." Denck's maxim also emphasized a knowledge of the living Christ.

A primary motif of discipleship for early Anabaptists was the call to suffering, or the "baptism of blood."[23] Given their frequent persecution, they developed a theology of suffering that impacted their hermeneutics. Murray believes that

> it is arguable that the Anabaptists, in their determination to take seriously the "hard sayings" of Scripture, tended to equate correct interpretations with those that demanded the greatest self-denial and suffering. (281)

Murray suggests that, at times, this ascetic approach may have distorted their interpretation. But modern adherents of the free church must not quickly look down their noses at the ascetic interpretations of those who have suffered for Christ. Martyrdom or willingness to die carries its own kind of authentication of scriptural interpretation.[24]

The discerning hermeneutic community must carefully balance the concepts embodied in the idea pair of discipleship vs. justification. An emphasis on discipleship, to the neglect of justification, courts several attendant dangers—legalism, humanism,[25] and lack of pastoral sensitivity.[26] On the other hand, an emphasis on justification, to the neglect of discipleship, can readily lead to antinomianism, cheap grace, and moral irresponsibility.

Again, the hermeneutic community which is overly concerned with discipleship may readily interpret the Scriptures to fit its own preunderstandings of obedience and its own human ability to comprehend, without due attention to the mystery of faith which justifies those who come to Christ in faith, seeking pardon from sin. Further, idealistic visions of discipleship, coupled with church authority, can lead to abuse and despair.[27]

However, leaving biblical ethical mandates undefined by practical considerations leaves Christians without a sufficient moral anchor. Hermeneutic communities who wish to bring healing and hope to the world cannot afford to neglect either discipleship or justification.

Word vs. Spirit

"The first mark of an Anabaptist approach to Scripture," writes Snyder (161), "is the insistence that the Spirit must inform any true reading of Scripture." On the other hand, Anabaptists have been known for their adherence to the "plain sense" of Scripture. So Anabaptist concerns about biblical interpretation relate both to the literal and the spiritual, or the emphasis on written revelation and on revelation made known by the Spirit of God. Murray maintains that Anabaptists were mostly in the middle of the "literal-spiritual" poles in biblical interpretation. Actually, they were accused of being at both ends. Generally, the Swiss Brethren were more likely to be accused of literalism, and the South Germans were more likely to be accused of spiritualism.[28]

The tension between Word and Spirit manifested itself in Anabaptist approaches to the relationship between the Old and New Testaments. Anabaptists believed that new revelation from the Holy Spirit had superceded the revelation recorded in the Old Testament. As Murray states,

> the New Testament was to be interpreted literally, because it was the reality, the essence, the fulfillment. The Old Testament was to be interpreted spiritually because its literal sense, though still historically important, was inapplicable. (175)

Snyder (161) argues that primitive "Anabaptist egalitarianism and anticlericalism" were rooted theologically and scripturally in the "spiritual" reading of the "letter" of Scripture. As time went on, however, the emphasis fell on "increasingly specific ethical and communal results of the Spirit's work," with specific communal tests to measure the authenticity of that work. These measures were defined by church elders and enforced by the ban. The charismatic nature of the early community was displaced by tradition and church discipline: "ecclesiology came to contain and define pneumatology" (368, 389).

In more recent times, some free church advocates in the charismatic tradition have emphasized *rhema* over *logos*,[29] believing that a *rhema* word constitutes a specific word from God through the ministry of the Holy Spirit, while *logos* stands for more general written revelation. Some interpretative communities, then, wait for a specific *rhema* word to give specific definition to their response to Scripture. Prophetic communities proclaim specific prophecies designed to give guidance to the church regarding the "current word of the Lord" or a particular application of Scripture. Some go so far as to claim Christian unity only with those who agree on the level of *rhema*, separating themselves from those who are not willing to obey a word revealed through particular prophetic utterances.[30]

The discerning hermeneutic community will do well to keep an emphasis on Word and Spirit in balance as they seek to do God's will. As Swartley (1983, 224) says, "Word and Spirit are at home with each other." Each "prophetic word" credited to the Spirit must be tested by Scripture. Again, obedience to specific commands of Scripture must be tested by the voice of the Spirit. Like the emerging church in the book of Acts, we must be alert to the movement of the Spirit in new and fresh ways. Any true discerning community requires both the presence and power of the Spirit, working through gifts given by the Spirit, and a commitment to the Bible, God's Word written. The discipline of Bible study, coupled with the co-creative work of the Spirit, can yield results far beyond that associated with intellectual pursuit alone.

Individual vs. community

Believers in the Anabaptist tradition hold a dynamic tension between individual and community. Many scholars, particularly those who value the hermeneutic community's role in biblical interpretation, tip their hand toward the hegemony of community. Kraus, for example, argues that one's identity is formed in community[31] (48). Miller (K and K) asserts: "In an Anabaptist vs. Mennonite perspective, the new life in Christ takes shape not only in the individual Christian, but fundamentally in the corporate reality of the Christian community amid an unbelieving world" (41).

Yet Anabaptist writers also show concern for individual gifting, expression, and participation, believing that the believing community must not undervalue the individual. At the same time, most of the writers who addressed this tension implicitly eschewed individualism as a bad thing.[32] Kraus distinguishes between individuality and individualism:

> The former calls attention to the individual as a responsible person in community, while the latter exalts the independence of individuals and their private rights. Individuality is affirmed in the form and content of the covenant; individualism is considered a matter of alienation and pride. (43)

The healthy hermeneutic community requires a careful balance between the individual and the community. Overemphasizing the former may lead to individualistic interpretations that undermine proper church authority,[33] accountability, or true communal discernment. Overemphasizing the latter may stifle individual creativity and the prophetic challenges which individuals may bring. The dialogical process in the discerning community should value what each person brings, yet tempering individualism by requiring some commitment to the community process. Perhaps the biblical image of the body of Christ (Rom. 12: 4-5; 1 Cor. 12:12-27) provides the best example of the balance in this idea pair.[34] Each part needs the body; the body needs each part.

Clergy vs. laity

Anabaptist studies over the past few decades have looked with disfavor on the common dichotomy between clergy and laity in Christian communions.[35] Further, the recent weight of emphasis has been on the empowerment of the laity. Yoder (1987) asserts that sixteenth-century Anabaptists ran against the mainstream with the concept of leadership, as did later Quakers and Plymouth Brethren. He says the latter two groups "have given the lie to those who assume that central clerical leadership is necessary to keep one's identity" (42).

In contrast to these radically egalitarian groups, however, shepherds (pastors) were appointed to lead in early Anabaptist communions. At the same time, the free church tradition has sought to empower all church members to fully participate in giving and receiving counsel, to use their gifts for ministry to others, and to help discern God's will in the congregation.

The biblical metaphor of the body points toward the need and value of all. The point of the passage in 1 Corinthians 12 and others seems to be that there is no hierarchy of gifts. All have the same source and each has equal value for ministry when exercised in their proper place. Yoder (1987) asserts that the term *laity*, defined as "those with no ministry"[36] is heretical and arises only generations after the Scripture was written (14). Ewert maintains that too much emphasis on the "separated" ministry militates against the lay apostolate (133). His perspective reflects an egalitarian stream of thought in the Anabaptist tradition.

On the other end of the idea spectrum, some churches in the free church community have swung toward an emphasis on apostleship as a particular "sphere of ministry" to be exercised in the contemporary church. Contemporary apostles, often linked with prophets, are perceived to be contemporary expression of the "five-fold ministry" spoken of in Ephesians 4:11. Apostles and prophets are translocal ministers that work with evangelists, pastors, and teachers to enable local congregations to "be built up" and "become mature," attaining to the whole measure of the fullness of Christ" (Eph. 4:13).

Designed to oversee local churches, apostolic ministries are patterned after New Testament models of ministry; particularly in the Pastoral Epistles,[37] apostles provide the translocal perspective which is so often missing in small fellowships of believers.[38] They work together with the local church to hear the mind of the Lord for a particular situation, believing that a hermeneutical community without an apostolic presence is not fully equipped to discern God's will. In contrast to egalitarian lay movements, churches that emphasize apostolic ministry tend to be hierarchical and authoritarian in nature. Women are generally excluded from the apostolic company, and apostolic directives, rather than group consensus, are employed in decision-making.

More recently, Anabaptist scholars have sought to hold the two poles of the clergy-laity dichotomy in greater tension with each other. Ewert, for example, sets forth a vision that includes both a high respect for the "separated" or "ordained" ministry and the hope that "the whole membership (men, women, and children) will become more conscious of their missionary calling, and will be encouraged *to be the church* in the diaspora" (133). And Miller suggests that "the recasting of authority, from the right to rule to the freedom to serve in a community of mutual subordination, is a biblical model which goes beyond the restoration of hierarchical structure, on the one hand, and egalitarian individualism on the other" (K and K, 116).

Discussions about the role of ordination for leaders often reflect ambivalence on this issue. Particularly as the church incorporates greater diversity into its membership, ordination for a broader range of persons tests the church's willingness to grant power and authority to those who have typically been disenfranchised. Consequently, questions of civil rights and social justice come to the fore. One reaction has been altogether to eschew ordination as a practice in the church.[39] Another reaction is to seek diversification in the pastoral office in keeping with the changing demographics in the church.

The clergy-laity polar pair has significant implications for participation in the hermeneutic community. Where there is a strong emphasis on the role of clergy, there is likely to be a corresponding neglect of the role of laity in discussions and discernment on matters of biblical interpretation. A strong emphasis on clergy authority, for example, can lead to strong hierarchical interpretations of Scripture with a corresponding emphasis on church rules and discipline, and unilateral decisions by leaders to excommunicate members or declare church doctrine.

An egalitarian approach, however, can lead to erosion of authority and a pluralistic approach to the Bible that makes it difficult to make good decisions. The discerning community, therefore, needs to keep in tension both the authority of pastoral leaders and the role of church members in the discussions and applications of the Scripture for contemporary life.

Scholarly contributions vs. unlettered contributions

Closely related to the clergy-laity distinction is the differentiation between scholars and those with less formal education. The early Anabaptists tended to be anti-intellectual. They didn't want their faith to be polluted by human reasoning or any human tendency to steer away from suffering. Murray contends that Anabaptists

> disagreed with the Reformers about the inability of uneducated people to interpret Scripture. They also disagreed with them about the influence of scholarship and higher

education, feeling that on balance such training did more harm than good, obscuring the meaning of Scripture rather than clarifying it. (73-74)

So while Anabaptists were eager to include even the weakest member in the process of biblical interpretation, they tended to exclude the educated scholars. They believed the only kind of reason necessary for interpreting Scripture was common sense, not knowledge gained through academic study. Therefore, they perceived education as

a greater hindrance to interpreting the Scripture than ignorance. Whether through necessity or prejudice, early Anabaptism failed to draw on theological and intellectual resources which could have enhanced the ability of its conegregations to engage in effective hermeneutics. (Murray, 253)

Today, even the Anabaptists' most ardent defenders agree that there was naivete among the Anabaptists. Their rejection of scholarship, for example, left them without adequate awareness of the witness of Christians in the generations that proceeded them. Murray contends that

Their ignorance of pre-Constantinian writers prevented them discovering how many of these held to interpretations of Scripture broadly similar to their own. It seems also that adopting an ecclesiology which in practice disenfranchised all but the present generation of Christians was unjustified and rather arrogant. (254)

In recent years, many Anabaptists have embraced biblical and theological scholarship as helpful to the church. Perhaps the pendulum has now swung to the opposite side of this idea pair, with a strong emphasis on the scholarly interpretation of Scripture. The challenge for the discerning hermeneutic community, therefore, is to properly balance the contributions of both scholars and those less formally educated. The apostle Paul asked, "Where is the scholar?" (1 Cor. 1:20), reflecting the relatively low social status of the primitive church.

As the church attempts to reach society today, it is imperative to include the poor and downcast along with the theologians and biblical scholars to help determine the meaning of

Scripture. As McKenna maintains, the good news is written for the poor, "those lacking the basic necessities for human living—food, clothing, shelter, education, medicine and health care, jobs, human dignity, and hope for the future" (220). These people must be taken into account when there is doubt or question about the meaning of Scripture.

A POLARITY MANAGEMENT APPROACH TO DIFFERENCES THAT ARISE IN GROUP PROCESS

Not all of the paradoxes or tensions that communal groups face have to do with theological or biblical differences. Some have to do with the dilemmas of ordinary life. Some of these can be managed by good process. Management, however, does not necessarily imply "control." Since even good group process is "messy" at times, managing can sometimes mean to "muddle through," or "make the best of it." There are, however, some perspectives that will help the group amid differences encountered in the group process.

The Concept of Polarities in Group Process

The term *polarities* is used here in a neutral sense, as explained by Barry Johnson. As a paradigmatic metaphor for polarity management, Johnson refers to the physical process of breathing. This activity involves a polarity consisting of two activities—inhaling and exhaling. Without *both* activities, breathing is impossible. So it is with all true polarities; both poles are as necessary as the two poles on a battery.

Johnson proposes that both poles, however, have an "upside" and a "downside." The stronger the emphasis on the "upside" of a pole, the more one experiences its "downside" as well. Take the common polarity of "conditional respect" vs. "unconditional respect." Whether in the church, at work, or at play, groups need both of these polarities. Johnson arranges the polarity into four quadrants as follows:

Upside of unconditional respect
- You love people for who they are
- Everyone has equal human rights
- Everyone is respected

Downside of unconditional respect
- Poor work is made equal to good work
- Problems are difficult to identify or correct
- People don't think of consequences

Upside of conditional respect
- Good work can be recognized
- You can point out and make needed corrections
- People learn to deal with consequences

Downside of conditional respect
- People are valued only for their work
- People may feel like "a number"

Johnson theorizes that when people experience the downside of one pole, they will naturally scramble to experience the upside of the other pole. If they succeed in a change of emphasis, of course, they will in turn experience the downside of that pole, and so on, in what is likely to be an ongoing cycle. The situation cannot be "solved" by a particular decision or action. If the problem can be "solved" in this way, it is not a true polarity. True polarities can only be *managed*. You cannot get away from the need for groups to be concerned about *both* conditional respect and unconditional respect *at the same time*. This polarity, it seems, is closely related to the "discipleship vs. justification" idea above discussed above. Discipleship places conditions on one's acceptance for salvation; justification proffers salvation without respect for persons—unconditional acceptance.

Congregations easily get tangled up in arguments about various polarities such as being/doing, faith/works, centralized authority/decentralized authority, and evangelism/nurture. In their book, *Managing Polarities in Congregations*, Roy Oswald and Barry Johnson show that when groups in discernment find themselves in an argument about *which* pole is more important, they easily lose sight of the essential nature of *both* poles. Since most members have a natural inclination toward (or some vested interest in) one pole or the other, they will tend to defend the importance of their own "pole" and disregard the importance of the other.

"Winning" this kind of argument can quickly lead to "losing" for everyone in the group. Either pole, when overemphasized or singled out, leads to negative results. Congregations that ignore this insight stand a good chance of getting stuck with the downside of one or both poles.

Congregational leaders have the challenge of managing polarities in such a way that both poles can function effectively in group life. Although you cannot emphasize both poles at the very same time (try inhaling and exhaling at exactly the same moment!) you can learn to swing back and forth between them in a relatively balanced manner. In this way, you can experience the upside of both poles without getting stuck on the downside of either or both.

For example, groups can show unconditional respect for church members by showing special care for members, regardless of their achievements or behavior. This means they can accept people just as they are (Rom. 15:7; unconditional respect). At the same time, they can honor members who have done excellent work (Rom. 13:7b) or confront members about behavior that is harmful or hypocritical (Gal. 2:11-12) demonstrating conditional respect. Both are essential to good group life. Amid a hermeneutical discernment process, one must balance the recognition of each person's contribution (unconditional respect) with the recognition that some have particularly helpful insights (conditional respect).

When groups encounter dilemmas that seem impossible to solve, they can apply the following two of Johnson's questions to ascertain whether or not they are dealing with a polarity: 1) Is the difficulty ongoing? 2) Are there two poles which are interdependent? If they answer yes to both questions, they may be dealing with a polarity.

Action Steps for Management of Polarities in Group Process

Johnson (135f.) suggests a number of steps that leaders can take as they seek to work effectively with polarities in group process:

1) They can identify the group's polarity.

2) They can lead the group into an activity that describes the four quadrants of a polarity. It is helpful to express the

"poles" of the polarity in neutral terms if possible, lest one or both sides appear to be pejorative.

3) They can diagnose which "quadrant" the group is experiencing now, and identify which individual or group is crusading for change and which are striving to keep things the same.[40]

4) They can predict the consequences (upside and downside) of moving in a particular direction.

5) They can prescribe guidelines for action, both for those who are trying to change the emphasis and those who are trying to maintain the status quo.

Also, groups can helpfully address three questions at times like these: 1) What do we want to achieve? 2) What do we want to preserve? and 3) What do we want to avoid? Although Johnson did not pose these particular questions, they fit well into his theoretical scheme. They also invite group participation in voicing both hopes and fears, two emotions that can significantly impact group discernment process.

A brief illustration from church life may prove helpful. One group of about a hundred persons gathered to discern a possible change of role description for the bishops in the leadership of their conference. After studying the history of and biblical basis[41] for the role of bishop, they explored the answers to these foregoing three questions in small groups gathered around tables in a large room. Then each small group reported back to the large group, with all of their responses being listed on a large sheet for all to see. Although this was a one-day event, it produced significant consensus on an issue that was potentially divisive. Participatory discussion, along with careful consideration of the various options and values, led to significant discernment and agreement.

A TRANSFORMATIONAL APPROACH TO CHURCH CONFLICT

Aside from the many biblical/theological tensions in communal discernment, frequently other tensions may result in significant conflict. In recent decades, social conflict theorists have produced a plethora of materials dealing specifically with church conflict. The overwhelming consensus among these authors is that conflict is normal and that one can learn to work constructively with conflict. Reflecting on the normalcy of differences in the average church, however, Prinzing prefers to speak of "tensions" as opposed to conflict. In his mind, conflicts have to do with "confrontation, friction, and competition," while tensions emphasize "stretching, growth, health, and balance." Appropriate tension adjustments can help prevent conflict.

When tensions escalate, however, groups may experience genuine conflict. They may even find themselves crippled by conflict, unable to move ahead with a meaningful discernment process. Particularly in the Anabaptist tradition, in which peacemaking is a high value, churches seek to transform conflict situations into peaceful ones. Therefore, it will be helpful to discuss briefly the ways that conflict may be transformed.

Conflicts readily move from their ideological or theological base to become interpersonal issues. Speed Leas (1982), the virtual dean of American church conflict mediation practitioners, explains that we all deal with contrasting urges—to be subordinate and cooperative on the one hand, and to be independent on the other. These urges lead to conflict. One does not simply move from dependence into autonomy, from support to control. One must stay at various places between the poles, depending on the situation. Leadership in these situations "demands the attention of the leader to the needs of the followers" (25). In conflict situations, the leader may need to help people on the support end of the continuum become more autonomous and assertive, and/or help the independent person submit his/her self interests to the interests of the group.

Leas affirms that leaders (particularly unbiased third parties) can help to *transform* the conflict situation by 1) empowering group members to use their best efforts in the conflict; 2) arousing confidence in the group and its leaders; 3) helping the group work toward common goals; and 4) providing or helping the group discover the means of achieving their goals. In transactional leadership,[42] the leader meets the people's needs from one time to the next. This may breed a sense of helplessness and cause persons to fight dirty. Transformational leadership empowers people and gives them confidence. By empowering others and encouraging them to stay in the conflict, the leader helps people deal with their fears and equips them for the future.

Types of Church Conflict in Discernment Processes

Church conflict theorists have categorized conflicts in a variety of ways.[43] For the purpose of focusing on discernment processes, we shall limit this brief discussion to just three—value conflicts, systemic conflicts, and personality clashes.

Value conflicts

The much-debated clash of values in society today is reflected in the church. In fact, church conflicts have the potential of being far more serious, because the church discusses eternal values. Differences that arise amid discernment processes typically are based on deeply held values. Sorting through differing values and finding ways to integrate them into an edifying, coherent system can pose a major challenge. Many of the ideas shared under polarity management apply here.

Systemic conflict

Building on a theory of differentiation proposed by Murray Bowen and Edwin Friedman, some church conflict theorists speak of systemic approaches to conflict resolution. Friedman's work is a departure from traditional notions of cause and effect in family therapy. Drawing insights from systems theory, he shows that the way that components (people, in this case) function within the system is influenced by their relationship to other components within the system. The interconnectedness of a system implies that every action taken by any member of a group will have a dynamic effect on the rest of the group. He shows how persistent relationship difficulties may often be traced to systemic issues introduced through unresolved difficulties in families of origin, whether they be lack of "differentiation," the formation of "emotional triangles," the draw toward "homeostasis," individual "overfunctioning" and "underfunctioning, " or "family secrets"—just to name a few of the issues. In turn, the church functions much like a family, with a system of its own.

Mitchell (32) explains that there are certain general principles of all systems. The most fundamental is that "systems behave as though they were persons with lives of their own." This

is played out in several ways: Systems 1) regularly act to preserve themselves and to resist change; 2) maintain both external and internal boundaries; 3) are always internally intercon-
nected; 4) assign specialized roles to their members; and 5) develop rules and rituals to bond members to one another and
thus to maintain and preserve the group.

Perhaps most significantly, Mitchell contends that when
there is major failure or conflict in a system, it is not wise to lay
blame on one individual's malicious intent. The system allowed it to happen. An individual who objects to what is happening but does not speak up is part of the system that allows
the behavior to happen (47). Leas says that unofficial roles per-
petuate themselves; if one complainer or challenger leaves a
group, for example, another one will quickly rise up to take the
role.

Systems theorists maintain that leaders have particular influence in systems. Leaders who learn to differentiate themselves from others in the system will have greater ability to understand the paradoxes in the system within which they find
themselves. They will have greater freedom to declare their
own positions without insisting that others do things their way,
and they can be a "non-anxious presence" amid conflict.

Mitchell insists that inevitably, when authority is thrown
out the front door, an authoritarian stance will creep in the
back. In the long run, it is best to define and place authority
within limits, not try to get rid of it (152). When outside facilitators are called into a conflict situation, they do well to examine systemic issues before proposing solutions.

Personality clashes

Sometimes two particular individuals have genuine difficulty getting along with each other. Their personalities simply
clash with each other, creating interpersonal conflict. If one or
both of these is influential in the church, their differences can
significantly impact an entire discernment process, particularly
if each looks for support from others.

More disturbing for many groups, however, is the challenge of dealing with difficult people.[44] Difficult people are not
necessarily emotionally disturbed but rather congregational
misfits. Marshall Shelley calls them "problem people" or "well-
intentioned dragons."

Kenneth Hauck shows that difficult people readily become antagonists.

> Antagonists are individuals who, on the basis of *nonsubstantive evidence, go out of their way* to make *insatiable demands*, usually attacking the person or performance of others. These attacks are *selfish in nature, tearing down rather than building up*, and are frequently directed against those in a leadership capacity." (25-6)

Antagonists particularly gravitate toward discussions of controversial church issues, perhaps seizing onto an issue as a way of avoiding the need to face their own intrapersonal conflicts. So, as Haugk contends, antagonists can become a "big fish" in small churches. People may mistake them for activists and follow them.

At times, the most loving way to deal with difficult people is to confront them with the truth—even though they themselves cannot see it. Confrontation is most effective when carried out gently and firmly. The principles presented in Matthew 18 are appropriate for situations such as these, bearing in mind that the process is designed for the purpose of reconciliation and restoration, not punishment or alienation.

However, it is seldom helpful for leaders to confront an antagonist in a public meeting. This breeds defensiveness and may be unwise for a number of reasons.[45] Therefore, the only time that public action is appropriate is for continuing, unconfessed actions or attitudes that the congregation clearly recognizes as sinful. For most situations, public action only further alienates the individual. Public rebuke may even galvanize some individuals to take up a public campaign against the church or its leaders.

Levels of Conflict

Leas (1985) identifies five levels of church conflict and gives a few symptoms of each. The two key identifying characteristics of each level of conflict are the parties' objectives and the way they use language. Each level reflects a higher level of group anxiety.

Of course, different individuals or groups within the congregation may be experiencing the conflict at a different level.

Basically, one can assume at least the level that the pastor is feeling or expressing. A brief explanation of the five levels follows.

Level One: Problems to Solve

At this level, parties engage in clear, specific language, oriented to the here and now. The parties are problem-centered, not people-centered. In other words, the issues have not become interpersonal in nature.

Level Two: Disagreement

Language begins to take on a more general level, describing a broader sense of mistrust or lack of communication. Parties become concerned about their own position and may draw others into the conflict, striving for self-protection.[46] The specific differences may be somewhat disguised by jargon.

Level Three: Contest

At this stage, the parties are concerned to demonstrate their own ascendancy and strength of position. People began clumping for support, but the boundaries are not hard and fast; there will still be connections with disagreeing parties. Nevertheless, both parties want to win the contest. Language becomes distorted through magnification, dichotomization, over-generalization, and arbitrary inference. There may also be a significant amount of irrational thinking.

Level Four: Fight/Fight

At this intense stage of conflict, parties not only want to win but to hurt the other. They become concerned primarily for the faction or subgroup of which they are a part, rather than the good of the whole. Language congeals into ideological categories, such as truth, freedom, and justice.

Level Five: Intractable Situations

Parties in this stage of conflict want to destroy or get rid of the other. They are no longer in control of the conflict. Language at this stage takes on eternal dimensions, with universal principles. The sixteenth-century Reformation illustrates this level of conflict in church history. Disagreeing factions in the church literally took up arms against each other. Anabaptists (particularly nonviolent ones) suffered at the hands of both Protestants and Catholics in the fray.

As noted in the introductory chapter, this study assumes relatively healthy congregations and low levels of conflict. Therefore, if the conflict escalates to level four, it will not likely be possible to function as an authentic hermeneutic community. Discernment will be clouded by strong emotions. Conflict at Levels Four and Five require intervention by outside church authorities to mitigate the damage that people in the conflict will do to each other.

The Role of Trained Facilitators

Any group discernment process may be enhanced by the leadership of a trained facilitator. Particularly when groups find themselves in conflict, trained facilitators can help transform the conflict. When groups in escalating conflict call for outside facilitators or neutral third parties, the language of "mediation" and "intervention" is appropriate.

There are a number of goals for mediation in church conflict.[47] These goals may perhaps be appropriately summed up in three mediatorial roles:

The *first role* is to help people think clearly about their options as they explore alternatives and manage polarities.

The *second role* is to help people gain hope, to help them believe that they have a future together, that they can define their relationship differently.

The *third role* is to work with systems or patterns of dealing with conflict.

The mediator may be able to help groups change entrenched, unhealthy conflict patterns. Like skilled leaders in discernment process, trained facilitators often implement steps to transform the conflict. They are outlined briefly below.

One of the first steps mediators take is to establish the ground rules by which participants interact with each other. In contrast to the tacit "rules" by which most groups function, ground rules clearly state expectations for group participation.[48] Sometimes mediators attempt to transform the conflict by enabling the group to name the tacit rules that are in operation. At times, to speak a rule aloud is to disarm it, particularly when a rule does not produce healthy group interaction. Stating the ground rules aloud at the beginning of the process provides both a framework for participation and public accountability for those who choose not to follow the rules.

After setting ground rules for interaction, facilitators can help the group to identify salient issues. This exercise can serve to separate substantial issues from interpersonal conflicts or secondary concerns. Mediators might be able, for example, to help the group identify and describe a particularly thorny polarity which has created conflict. In any conflict situation, issues easily become conflated with each other, or identified with particular persons. Skillful facilitators help to sort through the "mess" and make sense of what is going on.

As part of the process of defining salient issues, facilitators generally seek to gather information in an organized way. Surveys, interviews, and group discussions all serve to provide information on the nature of the conflict. While intuitive facilitators may be able to correctly assess the nature of the problems, experienced mediators base their work on a foundation of factual information. There is no adequate substitute for knowing the facts as well as the dominant perceptions of the issue.

Inevitably, facilitators must deal with power differences amid group discernment, particularly when disparities of power are in evidence. Because this aspect of group life is often overlooked, a more extensive discussion of this aspect of facilitation is in order here. First of all, two definitions are in order: *Power* is the ability of one party to control or influence another party in some way; *authority* is the delegated right to exercise such power. Leaders have both power and authority. If they had neither, they would not qualify to be called leaders.[49]

In addition to natural influence or delegated authority, leaders and others have some degree of *social* power simply by belonging to certain groupings within society. Consider the pairs in the columns below, representing persons who may all be participating in any particular hermeneutic discernment process. Although not *all* persons in the groups represented in the right-hand column are less powerful than *all* persons represented in the corresponding groups in the left column, these pairs convincingly portray reality as the majority experience it. The more groups with which one can identify in the left column, the more socially powerful one will be.

Powerful	Less Powerful
Adults	Children
Men	Women
White	People of Color
Wealthy	Poor
Supervisors	Workers
Bishops	Pastors
Clergy	Lay
People without a disability	People with a disability
Born in U.S.	Recent immigrants to U.S.
Formally educated	Not formally educated
Articulate	Inarticulate
Born in well-respected families	Born in little-known families
Teacher	Student

Christian leaders often feel a sense of powerlessness in the face of difficult circumstances. Consequently, they may be tempted to deny the immense social power that they can exercise in the lives of others. They may even feel threatened by persons with less power who challenge their position or aspire to their office. They may abuse their power.[50]

And yet, people who understand their power may be the most helpful in group process. As Bossart asserts, power need not be used for individual aggrandizement but can be expended for the mobilization of one's life resources for the goals of the group. The release of this kind of creative power enables integrative approaches to conflict management in the church. Mediators can help groups to acknowledge the power differences that exist within their group, call on people to use their power in helpful ways, and sometimes to "level the playing field" in such a way that the discernment process is more inclusive.

After gathering information and helping participants interact with each other, facilitators help group members generate possible "solutions" to their conflict. As noted above, some conflict does not yield to particular solutions but rather to definition, description, and/or clarification. Solutions generated by group members themselves work better than those suggested by facilitators. It is hoped that the group can come to a resolution which will help each person to feel that they have gained something crucial in the process.

Conflicts may be considered resolved when there is significant agreement in a particular direction. That may be either a specific decision, a definite plan, or significantly increased commitment to work together in harmonious ways.

The Ultimate Goal of Reconciliation

Some church conflicts leave participants wounded and alienated. At times, forging specific agreements or moving ahead with the majority may leave unfinished business amid the discerning group. Ideally, the goal of mediation in church conflict is to achieve transformation, so that both the persons and the situation lead to reconciliation. As Lynn Buzzard and Laurence Eck say, "to resolve issues but leave persons essentially unchanged—unforgiving, isolated, unaware of the peace of Christ—is not an adequate mission for Christian peacemakers" (52). And Ronald Kraybill, a mediator and practitioner in the Anabaptist tradition, asserts that peacemaking and reconciliation[51] lie at the heart of the Christian message.

Often however, the path to reconciliation is paved with pain. Bossart maintains that "conflict is as essential to Christian faith as the cross" (95). Further, "no fulfilling change seems to come about without this movement from chaos and disorganization to resolution and reconciliation" (96).

Leas (1985) rightfully builds on the theological premise that reconciliation, so prized in the church, is really a gift. Thus reconciliation does not work best as an operational goal, even though it is a meta-goal, or an ultimate goal. McSwain and Treadwell agree that the way of peace does not come easily. They posit that while the doctrine of Creation affirms the vision of a conflict-free existence, the doctrine of the Fall shows that humankind turned away from that vision. The source of conflict is sin in the created order.

The doctrine of salvation is the reconciliation of conflict. By encountering conflict, and conquering it, Jesus Christ gives us reconciliation. The way of reconciliation is acceptance of the supreme symbol of human conflict, the cross. The doctrine of the end points out the final consummation which comes through the obedience of Jesus. There will be a resurrection into an eternal kingdom, where the joys of creation will again be realized.

122 DISCERNING GOD'S WILL TOGETHER

Leas (1980) cites Matthew 18 and Luke 17 to show that repeated attempts must be made to reconcile to one's brother. However, he also cites other sayings in the Gospels which indicate that reconciliation will be impossible, such as the sayings about shaking the dust off one's feet and going elsewhere (Matt. 9, Luke 10).

Reconciliation is based on voluntary forgiveness. Not all will find themselves able to forgive, since one's capacity to forgive is related to one's "apprehension and appropriation of God's forgiveness" (Buzzard and Eck, 57). There are indeed limits to what persons or groups in conflict can achieve.

A Disclaimer Regarding the Limits of Conversation

Dialogue is a wonderful gift to experience amid a group. Genuine dialogue provides an opportunity to share feelings, perceptions, and thoughts in a safe environment. It can help to "sharpen"[52] conflict by clarifying different values, assumptions, or beliefs held by the parties in conflict. It will not, however, necessarily lead the parties to change. Some viewpoints or approaches are simply irreconcilable. Groups must then decide if both viewpoints may co-exist in the same fellowship. If not, dialogue may lead to a decision to part ways.

Again, sometimes corporate "angst" is simply too high for genuine dialogue to take place. While mediators may seek to reduce fears and engage people in conversation, other factors may keep the anxiety high. For example, the group may experience the trauma of loss amid a discernment process—the loss of a pastor, the unexpected death of an influential member, financial disaster, or the withdrawal of a group from the church. While it may be healthy for opposing parties to converse at such times, it may be unrealistic to hope to resolve major discernment issues at the same time.

Some persons amid discernment may resist dialogue because it seems to privilege the party pressing for change. Dialogue often moves discerning groups toward more diversity, more need for tolerance. Since educated people in general may be more articulate and tolerant than unlettered people, they may find those with less formal education resisting their proposals. This has certainly been true in many of the more conservative expressions of the Anabaptist tradition.

In sum, dialogue assumes the ability to deal with differences. Therefore, pluralistic groups with high tolerance for diversity will find dialogue most helpful. But, as McSwain and Treadwell have argued, conflict easily shatters a group that finds its identity in nonconformity to the surrounding culture. Members depend on each other for support in their nonconformist stance. When dialogue moves toward differentiation, they lose the sense of support and closeness they feel they need. This may explain why many groups in the free church tradition would rather "quit than fight."[53]

SUMMARY

In this chapter I have attempted to show that differences are a normal part of any communal process. Preparing for those differences and recognizing their worth can go a long way toward facilitating healthy processes of dialogue on difficult issues. Communal discernment often involves making difficult choices between competing values. Therefore, a dialectical approach to ideological tensions and a polarity management approach to differences in the church can help to develop a healthy, balanced strategy for making difficult decisions. At the same time, calling on the services of trained facilitators can help when conflict goes beyond what a local church can readily handle.

NOTES

1. This study has examined effects of modernization on Anabaptist scholars. Some see postmodern culture as moving in the opposite direction. For example, see Brueggemann (6), who (citing Toulmin) suggests that we are moving from written to oral, from universal to particular, from general to local, and timeless to timely. He suggests a new approach to biblical texts that will work in this changing framework.

2. Snodgrass suggests four primary tensions within persons: 1) saint and sinner, 2) pride and humility, 3) strength and weakness, and 4) authority and submission. He sees Christian faith in terms of tension as well: 1) faith and works, 2) grace and law, 3) freedom and responsibility, 4) God's activity or passivity, and 5) the Christian's being in the world but not of it.

Snodgrass sees three primary tensions of the Christian life that are foundational to the others: gift and task, the new age and the old, and a life patterned on both the death and the resurrection of Christ (16-7).

3. Snodgrass rejects the critical notion that an apparent tension within a biblical text is a sign of a later addition.

4. See Swartley (1983, 185-9) for his discussion of differing interpreting approaches to texts that present diverse perspectives on the role of women.

5. Swartley (1983, 217) objects to James Barr's image of a battlefield of conflicting ideas in the Bible but suggests that "at least we must recognize that the Bible is something like an orchestra, in which there are different instruments, blending usually, to be sure, but making distinctly different sounds."

6. For example, Walton argues that the emotional emphasis of Montanism in the second century was countered by the rationalism of Gnosticism in the second and third centuries, which in turn was countered by the emotionalism of Monasticism in the third to tenth centuries, until the onset of Scholasticism in the eleventh to fourteenth centuries, and so on (78).

7. One of the chief characteristics of postmodern thought is the emphasis on perspectives as opposed to the search for absolutes, as was common in modernism, which was based on scientific thought.

8. Karl Marx popularized Hegel's method of logic; it is based on the concept of the contradiction of opposites (*thesis* and *antithesis*) and their resolution in a new *synthesis*.

9. Commonly debated idea pairs might include 1) divine sovereignty and human free will, 2) God's justice and God's mercy, and 3) faith and works as evidence of Christian commitment.

10. Some consider "complementarity" a euphemism for "hierarchy," the view that God has ordained men to serve "headship" roles in family and church, with complementary submission on the part of women.

11. Anabaptists took membership in the church seriously, referring to their association as a covenanted body rather than as a "church." Cornelius Krahn (1981 255) explains:

> The designation "church" was not acceptable since the covenanters had just left the "'church' and dit [sic] not care to be identified with anything that would remind them of what they had left—even the name. So deep-seated was this objection that the Dutch Mennonites to this day use the term *gemeente* (*Geiende*, congregation) in speaking of their churches and the term *kerk* (*Kirche*, church) in speaking of the state church.

12. This term was used (perhaps coined) by Shank, 1988, 29.

13. Miller (K andK, 87) states:

> Rather than equating the church with the kingdom it would be better theologically to speak about the church as community of the kingdom in the midst of and in dynamic interaction with the world. This would correspond more closely to the biblical descriptions of the kingdom and its relation to the church and the

world. This distinction could also help correct the tendencies to misconstrue the primary role of the church in relation to the kingdom in ways which have been typical of Constantinian Christendom. In addition, this clarification could also help correct tendencies which have often arisen among Christians to justify withdrawing from witness and ministry in the world by limiting the agenda of the kingdom to the internal concerns of the church.

14. The Puidoux conference in Europe, and a strategy for witness to the state that arose out of it, were built on the concept of "middle axioms." Participants in the conference made the following declarations:

> Love constrains us to action for justice and peace among men with all our strength, by every means compatible with the Gospel, and therefore without recourse to war.
>
> The Lordship of Christ signifies for Christian ethics that the "good" is one: there are not two separate and unrelated realms or criteria in the church and in the world.
>
> When the state wages war in spite of the witness of the church against its use, the church does not become silent, but rather continues to testify as to the way in which this violence is used. In its criticism of political events the church will guide itself by criteria which translate into political terms the directives of the Word of God. These criteria ("middle axioms"), such as retributive and distributive justice, are valid measures for relative judgments, even though they fall short of the righteousness of God and therefore may not be determinative for Christian discipleship. (*Puidoux Theological Conference*, 1956, 57)

The discussions at Puidoux represented an act of dialectical transcendence. Whereas two-kingdom theology carved out separate realms of ethics for church and world, the new formulations transcended this dissociation by declaring the "Lordship of Christ over Church and State." This act of rhetorical boundary work declared Jesus Christ as sovereign over the affairs of the *whole* world, placing *both* church *and* state under the same ultimate authority. So, while church and state remained distinct in some respects, they were joined in the sense that Christ was Lord over both entities.

With this new theological formulation, it became the Christian's responsibility to bear witness to Christ's lordship over the state. Part of that witness was the testimony to the state that it must yield to Christ's authority, living up to the ethical standards in the Bible. Knowing that the state would not readily acknowledge Christ's authority, conference participants suggested that when the state rejected their witness, they could continue to testify by means of *middle axioms*, such as "retributive and distributive justice."

15. (Cf. Matt. 13:24-30; 19:23; 25:1-13; Mark 10:14; Luke 8:16; John 18:36).

16. Darby divided Biblical time (past and future) into seven dispensations, or epochs, each characterized by different ways that God re-

lated to people. Premillennialists believe that a rapture will take God's people out of the world before the millennium, a literal reign of Christ on the earth for 1000 years.

17. Kraus (92) declares that

> there is only one gospel of Christ, and it is the "gospel of the king-dom." Christ is both message and the messenger. As message he is the one in whom the authoritative presence and power of God unto salvation becomes reality. As messenger he proclaims the rule or kingdom of God—announcing that in a decisive, new way God's presence and power are manifest among us.

18. Kraus (88) argues that the church is central in God's plan for the salvation of the world. "The kingdom is manifest as the rule of Christ in the church, and individuals experience that saving rule as they partici-pate in the "community of the king."

19. Redekop contends that "The Christian church has been seduced into thinking that its social form is its transcendental nature" (48).

> All evidence suggests that the Christian church has normally been seduced and captured by the spirit of its age. Rather than speaking out in the prophetic voice, the representative of the tran-scendent reality, it has been the perpetrator of evils in total contra-diction to its purpose and profession. (70)

20. Redekop (77) asserts,

> The conviction that every decision must be made in the context of life in the kingdom of God can easily be taken as a definition of sacralization, or the opposite of secularism. The Mennonite tradi-tion has struggled to keep this concept of the life in the Kingdom of God alive, although it has fallen into the trap of legalism so often and so seriously that the Mennonite tradition has often been dismissed as idealistic groups unworthy of serious attention.

21. "A direct connection between the church and the kingdom of God is undermined by concepts of eschatology which separate ethics from eschatology." This happens when theologians, attempting to downplay the role of human action, conceive of eschatological action as "unilateral divine action which ends history in contrast to human ac-tion in history." (Miller in K and K, 88).

22. Yoder (1954, 45-6) conceived of discipleship

> as denoting a particular attitude toward the Christian life, whose major emphases are: (a) That the Christian life is defined most ba-sically in ethical terms. While forgiveness, membership in a social order, participation in worship, or receiving a revelation may all be very relevant factors, they do not rob *obedience in ethics (Nach-folge)* of primary rank. (b) That valid ethical instructions are given in the New Testament, on the basis of which we may reliably know the precise content of the obedience which is expected of us.

23. Anabaptists taught three true baptisms: (1) the baptism of the

Spirit, (2) the baptism of water, and (3) the baptism of blood.

24. "Willingness to die" for one's interpretation stands in stark contrast to "willingness to kill" for one's interpretation. In the end, the major Reformers as well as the Catholic Church enforced their biblical interpretation with the sword. This does violence to the word of God.

25. Levi Miller (34) asserts that modern Anabaptism has lost much of its original evangelical thrust, just as the Quakers have lost their Puritan Christian center. In Miller's mind, this movement was abetted by Robert Friedmann, an Anabaptist scholar of Austrian descent. Friedmann worked at Goshen College, organizing historical materials. He negatively contrasted "sturdy Anabaptism" with "sweet Pietism," attempting to drive a wedge between these two emphases. Miller maintains that Friedmann's book, *The Theology of Anabaptism*, may be best understood as a Tolstoyan reading, defining Anabaptism primarily as existential Christianity. Against this reading, Miller advocates for "an evangelical Anabaptism" that "embraces both the blessing and the scandal of the Apostles Creed and Jesus' Sermon on the Mount."

26. Steve Dintaman argues that neo-Anabaptism, following Harold Bender, introduced a theological reorientation which has profound pastoral implications for recent generations. "The first movement in neo-Anabaptist pedagogy is a dislocative or deconstructive move where the taken-for-granted theological concepts—and even more the theological priorities—of evangelical Protestant theology had to be unlearned" (37). Dintaman observes that theories of vicarious atonement were said to militate against discipleship and expressions of "community" tended to displace the work of the Holy Spirit in individual lives. What is most troubling for him is that Anabaptist pedagogy dislocated students without firmly planting them in "something that was both more biblical and at the same time deeply a part of their own experience and life" (39).

27. Roth (1995 60) proposes a model of church life drawn from Philippians 3:10-14, 16 that holds forth an ideal, knowing that one may spend a whole lifetime trying to reach it. He calls this "living between the times." "True Christian identity, Paul seems to suggest, is forged out of a holy tension between past and future; between what used to be and what is still to come; between the memory of an all-too-human history and the anticipation of a future heavenly perfection." To live between these times, Roth suggests, is the essence of Christian faithfulness.

28. Murray (193) contends,

> Among Anabaptists, Mantz and Grebel (and most of the early Zurich group) should be placed on the literalist edge; Hut, Denck, Kautz and Bunderlin (and many of the South and Central German groups), on the spiritualist edge. Among the Swiss, Hubmaier and Sattler both displayed a more moderate approach than their Zurich colleagues. The centre ground was probably held by the Dutch leaders, Menno Simons and Dirk Phillips, and by the German groups associated with Marpeck and Scharnschlager.

29. *Rhema* and *logos* are both English transliterations of Greek words that are translated as "word" in the New Testament.

30. But Watson (111) states that "the massive weight of evidence shows that there is no clear distinction to be made between *logos* and *rhema* in the Scriptures."

31. Kraus maintains that in Israel, the individual's relationship to God was not submerged in group identity, as it was in some ancient cultures. Each person had a unique responsibility to God. This stands in sharp contrast to New Age teaching today, where individuality and identity is grounded in nature.

32. Yoder (1984, 24-5) argues that Western intellectualism swings wildly between the individual and the collectivity. Radical Protestantism can show a third way between these two. "The alternative to arbitrary individualism is not established authority but an authority in which the individual participates and to which he or she consents. The alternative to authoritarianism is not anarchy but freedom of confession." "The moral validity of a choice one makes is connected to the freedom with which one has first of all made the choice to confess oneself a disciple of Jesus and to commit oneself to hearing the counsel of one's fellow disciples."

33. "It is in a proper understanding of the gifted community that our concept of authority among believers emerges. Here a course is steered between the democracy of majority rule and the authoritarianism of minority rule. The gifts of the spirit remove the idea that everyone is equally able to play every role" (Lederach, 132-133).

34. H. S. Bender (1962, 26) discusses Paul's use of the metaphor of the body of Christ:

> Behind the image of the body is the Hebrew notion of corporate personality. The pronounced individualism of our Western culture today, resting as it does upon Greek thought, makes it difficult for us fully to grasp this idea. For the Hebrew the individual existed only as a particular expression of the total people; his character was determined by solidarity with all others of his people. His people were prior to himself as an individual.

35. John Howard Yoder particularly, but Ross Bender, J. Lawrence Burkholder, John Driver, and others addressed the clergy-laity polarity in their writings.

36. John H. Yoder (1987, 6)contends that most religions, indeed churches, have a "religious specialist." But he asserts that there is no New Testament warrant for the following practices: 1) "one particular office 2) in which there should be only one or a few individuals 3) for whom it provides a livelihood 4) unique in character due to a ritual of ordination 5) central to the definition of the church 6) and the key to her functioning."

37. But Yoder (1987) asserts that one cannot justify apostolic monarchical leadership based on the Pastoral Epistles. Some do, arguing that

since these epistles were written later, they show development toward hierarchy (24). Yoder counters their argument by saying that the churches were younger, so they needed stronger leadership. Timothy was moving out of, not into, a monarchic role. The other churches whom Paul visited had been self-governing for years (26). He concludes: "Thus the figures of Timothy and Titus demonstrate not yet the rise of the resident bishop but the survival into the second generation of the role of the authoritative church-planting itinerant (27)."

38. Apostles and prophets sometimes gather in clusters to encourage one another and hear the current word of the Lord for specific geographic regions, both large and small.

39. Yoder (1987) makes the point that the clergy system militates against social justice. The current system of ordination tends to exclude women, minorities, the poor, the untrained. However, rather than encouraging these classes of people to break into the system, he suggests they stay out of it. "When a role has been defined on dominion-oriented grounds in the first place, why should a ministering woman want that status?" (51). "The wrong way to work at the agenda of women in ministry is the way most people are currently working at it, namely be a politicized, polarized struggle to open the closed ranks of the tiny clerical minority to admit the ordination of a few clergy of the opposite sex" (52). "The equal dignity of every ministering person in the body of Christ is not a distant goal to be attained by transforming the whole culture through a long process of corrective education. Rather, it is a fact to be appropriated by faith in the empowering work of the Holy Spirit" (53). "The same ought to be and can be the case for all other lines of diversity; for ethnicity, class, skills, education" (53).

40. Johnson (55) uses the terms *crusaders* and *tradition bearers* to describe these two forces. The former are trying to move from the downside of the currently emphasized pole to the upside of the opposite pole. The latter are attempting to maintain the upside of the present pole and avoid the downside of the opposite pole.

41. Discernment in older social groups works better when it involves a study of their tradition as well as the Biblical base for the tradition. Group members may well have conflated the two sources of their current practice, identifying their tradition too closely with Scripture. Looking at the changes in practice throughout their history can help to differentiate between the two at points.

42. Transactional models of leadership tend to seek resolution through trade-offs and compromise, rather than through transformation of the people and the situation.

43. Finrow, for example, identifies five types of conflict in the local church:

1) Relational—including both intrapersonal conflicts and interpersonal conflicts

2) Limited resources—such as space, money, property, and workers.

130 DISCERNING GOD'S WILL TOGETHER

3) Preferences—having to do with tastes or opinions

4) Values—such as theological convictions, ethical positions, and priorities for ministry

5) Organizational conflict—clash of roles, departmental conflicts, and environmental factors such as room arrangements.

Shawchuck gives examples of three types of conflict in the Bible: 1) over purposes and goals, 2) over programs and methods, and 3) over values and traditions.

44. Robert Dale's six categories of difficult people are: 1) the lonely church member, 2) the clique in the church, 3) the non-communicating crazymaker, 4) the hostile, 5) the apathetic church member, and 6) the traditionalist.

45. According to Haugk, it may 1) give the antagonist undue attention and recognition, and reinforce bad behavior; 2) be perceived as taking unfair advantage of one's leadership position; 3) create doubt in the minds of the congregation where there was none; 4) create an unhealthy atmosphere for the whole congregation; 5) portray the leader as an ogre; and finally, 6) violate the use for which the public channels were intended.

46. Leas offers a list of ways for facilitators to impart hope in the midst of conflict, primarily when the conflict is at Levels One and Two:

Experience corporate worship, especially singing

Explore possibilities for the future

Name the strengths of the church

Do Bible study

Discuss the church's conflict values

Use a consensus-building technique

Document the *range* of viewpoints; move beyond polarities

Share stories of successes in similar circumstances

Pray together, allowing people to hear God and share feelings

Ask what is the worst that could happen

Allow free talk; listen to each other (this can lead to venting and catharsis)

47. Leas suggests the following goals for an intervention:

tension reduction (find hope and safety)

vision for the leadership team

build trust

raise hope

help people feel good about themselves

solve problems

experience at least a small success

identify next steps

empower the primary leader

48. Following is a set of ground rules that may be used at a particular group discernment process. They should be stated at the outset of the meeting.

Only one person will speak at a time.

Wait to speak until you have been acknowledged by the moderator.

Use a microphone (the group comprised more than 100 people)

Speak only for yourself, unless you name the specific persons for whom you are speaking

If you wish to register a complaint about the group process, be specific about the time, place, and behavior which is offensive to you

Please do not applaud when someone says something with which you strongly agree. This behavior tends to polarize rather than unite the group.

Please keep your comments brief and focused. The moderator will reserve the right to limit your time.

49. Cf. Turner (26-7), who asserts

> Images of people who have power but not authority haunt the imagination. Images of people who have authority but not power are harder to come by. Indeed, it is probably the case that no such images exist because authority with no power at all is both a logical and impractical impossibility.

50. When the church has striven for and achieved social and political influence, it has inevitably used that influence to force conformity on the people with less power. As Philip Yancey (92) observes,

> The peaks of success and earthly power [in church history] . . . mark the peaks of intolerance and religious cruelty, the stains of church history we are most ashamed of today. It is as though love cannot coexist with power, and success contains within it the guarantee of a crash to come.

51. Leas and Kittlaus contend that because of a strong desire for reconciliation, ministers are generally unable to "referee" conflicts in their own churches.

> First, most ministers perceive reconciliation as leading to a peaceful church which is distinguished by the absence of conflict. What is really going on in this situation is the repression of conflict for the sake of peace. This may be called reconciliation, but it is only a cease-fire. (73).

52. In church conflict, sharpening conflict is generally a good step toward resolution. Until there is adequate differentiation between the issues, a clear resolution will not be possible.

53. I use the word *fight* to stand for verbal sparring. David Augsburger found that one sample of Anabaptist Mennonites "indicated an extremely low incidence of assaultive and verbal hostilities which are positively correlated with conscientious objection and high nonresistance values" (148).

CHAPTER 5

CONTEMPORARY HERMENEUTIC COMMUNITIES OF DISCERNMENT

*T*HE CHURCH OF JESUS CHRISt, even in its most local expression, is much more than a hermeneutic community or even a community of discernment. Biblical interpretation and discernment, albeit essential, are only two of the many functions of church life. It seems appropriate, then, to weave the vision for discerning hermeneutic communities into the broader fabric of the church. That is the purpose of the first half of this chapter. In this section, more than any other in this study, I will present my own perspectives and convictions. The second half of the chapter looks at ways in which the discerning hermeneutic community functions at various levels in the church.

A VISION FOR DISCERNING HERMENEUTIC COMMUNITIES

At the core of the free church lies the commitment *to be and make disciples of Jesus Christ.* A compelling allegiance to the kingdom of God under the lordship of Jesus Christ governs the lives of church members both individually and corporately. In its corporate form, the faithful church expresses this basic commitment in three integrally connected spheres—worship, community, and mission.[1] The vision for a discerning hermeneutic community is fruitfully expressed both in the core commitment to discipleship as well as each of these three practical spheres, as set forth below.

Commitment to Jesus Christ as Lord

The church helps to advance the kingdom of God by bringing everything under the authority of Christ, just as Jesus demonstrated his own obedience to God by dying on the cross (See Heb. 5:7-10, Col. 1:15-22). In my mind, commitment to obedient discipleship is the touchstone for faithful interpretation of the biblical text. It lies at the heart of faithful discernment amid the community.

Certainly, unbelievers or the marginally committed may understand the biblical text as literature and may receive its wisdom to some extent. But I question whether they can fully comprehend or experience its life-giving message without the passion for discipleship coursing through their veins. They will not be able to discern God's ultimate will for their lives and the lives of others. "Because Jesus Christ is the Word become flesh, Scripture as a whole has its center and fulfillment in him" (*Confession of Faith*, 21).

As those who have demonstrated their commitment to Jesus Christ through faith and baptism, church members turn to the Scriptures with gratefulness and expectation. As stated in a current confession, "The Bible is the essential book of the Church" (*Confession*, 22). "Through the Bible, the Holy Spirit nurtures the obedience of faith to Jesus Christ and guides the church in shaping its teaching, witness, and worship" (*Confession*, 22). "All other claims to represent an authoritative word on matters of faith and life must be measured and corrected by Scripture through the guidance of the Holy Spirit in the community of faith (*Confession*, 23). The church delights in hearing, reading, studying, marking, learning, and meditating upon the Scriptures, for they tell of Jesus Christ and show the church how to live fully and freely in his presence.

Further, I believe that a commitment to Jesus Christ, with its corresponding commitment to discipleship, has many implications for the practical life of the church, namely its expressions in worship, community, and mission. These implications are explored briefly under these three headings below.

Worship

The church's identity as people of faith—as followers of Jesus Christ—is sustained and renewed as its members gather for worship. In worship, "the church celebrates God's boundless grace, reaffirms its loyalty to God above all else, and seeks to discern God's will" (*Confession*, 40). "At the center of Christian worship is an encounter with the Word of God—both the living Word (the presence of the risen Christ among us) and the written Word of Scripture" (*Congregational Discipling*, 20).

Biblical interpretation and discernment are integrally woven throughout the fabric of the worship practices of the faithful church. In the free church, the Bible is "the authoritative source and standard for preaching and teaching about faith and life, for distinguishing good and evil, and for guiding prayer and worship (*Confession*, 21). The worship of the church (hymns, prayers, rituals, ceremonies, and other activities) may be shaped in various ways by Scripture. However, it seems appropriate to expand briefly on two areas—preaching and public reading of Scripture.

Although worship practices vary considerably from one congregation to another in the free church, preaching remains a central task. Preaching is one of the best ways to equip the church to become as a discerning hermeneutic community. Expository[2] preaching is the ideal, since it takes the Scripture seriously and models both interpretation and discernment for the community of faith. At the heart of expository preaching, as defined here, is the preacher's desire to "expose" the meaning of the text; to open up oneself to the authority and contemporary relevance of Scripture. "Ultimately the authority behind preaching resides not in the preacher but in the biblical text" (Robinson, 23). Sermons in the faithful church are significantly "shaped by Scripture" (See Wardlaw).

Expository preaching takes into account both the content and the context of biblical passages. It uses the tools of exegesis to discover the meaning of the text for its original hearers. It seeks to discover the timeless, universal truths in a text which may inform contemporary hearers. It organizes the ideas around a central theme or plot that helps to carry the meaning. It may employ narrative, explanation, rhetorical strategies, and applications in an effort to convey the meaning of the text. It seeks both to demonstrate God's provision for those who desire to follow God's way (grace) and to persuade the listener to obey the truth of the text (judgment).

Expository preaching has to do not only with the biblical text but with Jesus Christ. "The heart of expository preaching is the gospel itself—the story of Jesus" (Hayden, quoted in Gresham 11). But it is more. "Building around the gospel, expository preaching needs to give orderly attention to the entire Bible" (Hayden 12). Only as a congregation becomes familiar with the whole of Scripture can they experience the full-orbed vision of God's will for humans essential for discernment.[3]

Along with expository preaching, the public reading of Scripture helps a congregation to achieve biblical literacy. Careful worship planning can create an opportunity for congregants to be exposed to all of the different genres of Scripture over a period of time, whether in a sermon or public reading. Public reading, often called "oral interpretation," is a dramatic form of biblical interpretation. Contemporary readers easily lose sight of the fact that much of the Scripture was written for public presentation to non-literate hearers.[4] In today's visual and aural culture, dramatic enactments of the Scripture can sometimes be a highly effective way of communicating the meaning of the written text. While the preaching task in a congregation is often vested in a clergy person, public reading and dramatic enactments open up interpretive opportunities to many others in the church.

Worship is not simply an opportunity for persons to hear God's word, to express themselves to God individually, or to receive personal inspiration from the Scriptures. Worship is a corporate activity, based on the nature of the church as the body of Christ. Corporate worship is a time when God may speak to the church in various ways, such as a testimony, a word of instruction, a prophecy, a tongue, or an interpretation (see 1 Cor. 14:26).

In some free church traditions, the sermon is followed by a time of "testimony," when several persons pass judgment on the sermon's faithfulness to Scripture. This tradition likely grew out of the apostle Paul's exhortation to "weigh carefully what is said" (1 Cor. 14:29). This tradition incorporates both biblical interpretation and discernment into its response to the sermon—an expression of the discerning hermeneutic community at work in each worship service.

There are many other ways, of course, in which the church expresses its corporate nature through discernment and biblical interpretation. We will now turn to the ways in which they may find practical expression in the church's life in community.

Community

The church is a community shaped by story—the biblical story. The contemporary church community is shaped, molded, and transformed as it participates in the ongoing drama of God's acts in history. The church is a guardian and a steward of the stories which shape its identity as the people of God, not only the biblical story but its own continuing story. It has been said that a church without a strong sense of its past may well have no future. It is the church's responsibility to interpret that Story, and those stories, in such a way that they edify or build up the church.

Because the nature of the church as community is discussed at some length in Chapter Two, the following discussion will look at more pragmatic considerations: What might biblical interpretation and discernment look like in the life of the church community?

First of all, the faithful church will shape and critique its vision and ministry on the basis of Scripture, interpreted by the power of the Holy Spirit. Perhaps primarily through a program of Christian education, the church sustains a corporate approach to life and mission. People will be guided in their study of the Bible in small groups, whether through bought curriculum or through inductive study. Bible memory work will be encouraged, particularly in the early years of a child's life. People will be quick to ask, "What does the Bible say?" not only on the level of individual meaning, but on the broader meaning for the group.

CONTEMPORARY COMMUNITIES OF DISCERNMENT 137

Second, the faithful church welcomes all who earnestly come seeking to know God. It provides a safe place where people can share deeply with one another—confessing their faults and praying for each other, to experience God's forgiveness, healing, and release. It provides a place for people to air their doubts without rebuke,[5] offering encouragement and hope. It seeks to provide support for persons with difficult circumstances, such as poverty, significant loss, disability, abuse, or mental and emotional distress.

In all of these ways and more, the church provides a safe place to explore the deep meanings of the Scripture in a context of mutual support and care. Without such a context of support, much of biblical interpretation and discernment will remain on the surface level of ideas, rather than embodying the transformational power of God.

Third, the church will give attention to cultivating the habits, attitudes, and skills of faithful biblical interpretation. By careful planning, the church can integrate its worship and community life in such a way that persons have a sense of purpose in their study. For example, sermon themes may complement the themes in Christian education classes or small groups.

Further, elective classes in Christian education can provide excellent training in basic interpretative skills. By studying principles of biblical interpretation, the church can equip its members to communally interpret the biblical text. In addition, the church can encourage (and perhaps financially support) some of its members to take formal courses in biblical interpretation. In turn, these members can teach what they have learned to others in the church.

Fourth, the faithful church deliberately cultivates the habits of listening for God's voice in the practical affairs of the church. Spirit-led churches provide opportunities for its members to share in significant discernment or decision making on a regular basis. They invite the Bible to "confront and transform current presuppositions, understandings, and commitments" (Dietterich, 2). When the leaders of the church invite and take seriously the feedback of its members on matters of church life, they have the reward of members who take strong ownership of the church's welfare.

Some churches choose their leaders and other workers through group consensus processes that comprise both the nominees for the role and those with whom they would work. Prayer and group discussion form the basis for discernment of gifts and calling to the task. Such processes teach members the importance of group discernment. They stand in contrast to processes of election or decision-making by voting. In matters of significance that have the potential to be divisive, churches may choose to invite trained facilitators to instruct and lead the church in the discernment process.

Finally, the church as a discerning interpretive community embraces the diversity of God people.[6] Specifically, the church seeks to hear the voices of those who have often been dispossessed or rejected by the church. In a society with a growing number of hate groups clamoring for recognition, the church must renew its commitment to embrace seekers despite race, class, sexual orientation, or ethnic origin.

Beyond that, the faithful church develops specific opportunities for members to experience community beyond the local church, such as the fellowship of a district, denomination, and/or the broader Christian church. Without a global perspective and a keen sense of mission that seeks to welcome the stranger, the church is handicapped in its efforts to faithfully interpret Scripture or discern God's will for today.

Mission

Early Anabaptists modeled the truth that the church must not be content to stay as a fellowship to itself. The purpose of the church is to bear witness to the good news of Jesus Christ. As God's people, the church reaches beyond its walls through witness, service and peacemaking. The church is called to be a missional society, a community called and sent by God into particular contexts with a message of salvation, healing, and hope.

The mission of the church, along with its worship and community life, is shaped by Scripture. At its heart, the Bible is a missionary book, reflecting God's desire that all should be saved and come to a knowledge of the truth (1 Tim. 2:4). From the call of Abram in the book of Genesis (12:1-3), God expressed the desire to form a people who would bless all the nations.

Through study of Scripture, churches can arrive at a corporate discernment of their mission in the world. Not unlike the early believers in the church at Antioch, they pray, fast, discern God's call, and commission workers in the context of the worshiping community (Acts 13:1-3).

I have observed that a common vision for mission is one of the most powerful unifying forces which a group can experience together. To really energize the church, a vision must grip the church, producing the confidence that *this vision* is what God desires for *this time* and *this place*. Renewal in the church is often preceded or accompanied by a fresh vision of what God desires. The discernment process of arriving at this mission either recaptures the original vision of the church or finds a new vision to propel the church forward in a common commitment. A church without a specific vision is like a traveler without a specific destination.

Since faithful churches are energized by their commitment to a specific vision, many churches find that drafting mission and vision statements help them in this task. A mission statement must be based on a biblical understanding of what the church corporately believes that it is called to be and do. There is perhaps no more strategic exercise in the church than to work together as a group to formulate a corporate vision, based on biblical study and communal discernment.[7]

Again, in the faithful church, biblical interpretation and discernment significantly undergird its corporate identity as an "alternative culture" within surrounding society.[8] Fundamentally, the biblical narratives provide a window on the world quite at variance with the contemporary milieu. Varied media flood contemporary homes with myths of "individualism, materialism, nationalism, racism, sexism, and a worldview which denies the reality of anything beyond the grasp of the five senses and reason" (*Confession,* 45). In this environment, the Bible provides a lens by which church members can rightly view the world in which they live. The missional church must rely on its biblical and theological resources to provide a holistic vision for a deeply troubled world.

Just as biblical interpretation requires exegesis of the biblical text, the missional vision requires exegesis of the social/cultural situation.[9] Wilson explains,

In interpreting the biblical text, the text illuminates our world, and our world critiques the text, in a continuing hermeneutical spiral until the appropriate understanding is found. Even as exegesis of the biblical text is necessary, exegesis of our situation is also necessary, or we cannot adequately interpret the text.

"Exegesis of our situation," Wilson elaborates, is "the evaluation of life around us from the perspective of a community that strives to be faithful to the Word, even as we constantly submit that community life to be under the Word" (161). Interpreting the text and discerning God's response in light of the cultural situation are crucial disciplines in the faithful church.

Finally, the missional church invites seekers to explore discipleship in the community of faith. Sincere seekers as well as newly converted disciples introduce an essential dimension into communal interpretive and discerning processes. They tend to challenge implicit assumptions, pose new questions, and seek immediate applications of Scripture. The transformation experienced by new believers can help to transform and enliven disciples who have follow Jesus for many years.

Summary

The foregoing study has assumed that the local church is the basic examplar of the hermeneutic community. Local, weekly assemblies[10] provide the spiritual stimulation, social interaction, and emotional support that is needed for successful discernment in matters of biblical interpretation. One cannot assume, of course, that every congregation provides all of these components in sufficient degree to function well as a hermeneutic community.

Furthermore, the church as a community exists not only in the local congregation but also as a community of congregations and as the worldwide community of faith. Consequently, it will be helpful to consider other contemporary forms of hermeneutic communities of discernment. In addition to holding membership in a local congregation, adherents in the free church may seek fellowship in one or more of the following networks that may function effectively in some dimension of hermeneutic discernment. The section that follows is primarily illustrative; it does not purport to be exhaustive.

CONTEMPORARY NETWORKS THAT FUNCTION AS HERMENEUTIC COMMUNITIES

Small Groups

Intentional face-to-face social groups provide interaction on a primary level. Therefore, small groups bring the strength of intimacy to the task of hermeneutical discernment. Primary groups provide a place for in-depth discussion and interaction that is simply not possible in large groups. Bible study can have its most transformative effect in such groups, particularly when group members are committed to loving accountability. Specific implications or practical applications of Scripture are likely to be the matter for discernment in such groups, with the experience of groups members figuring prominently in the process. However, when members "stay in their heads" rather than sharing from the heart, small group discussions do not hold much of an advantage for discernment over the large group experience.

Area/Denominational Clusters

Many congregations in the free church tradition affiliate at some level beyond the local church in an area or denominational association. The Mennonite church, for example, sees such affiliation as a vital part of the church: "The church exists as a community of believers in the local congregation, as a community of congregations, and as the worldwide community of faith" (*Confession*, 40). Such groups commonly have confessions of faith or statements of policy on controversial issues.

Two denominational groups in the Mennonite tradition adopted the confession of faith just cited,[11] and it continues to be used by their reconfigured successors, Mennonite Church USA and Mennonite Church Canada. Their process for testing and revising the draft document illustrates one form of hermeneutical community. Seeking feedback, the joint committee which drafted the initial document made copies available to any congregation in both denominations upon request. The committee was surprised and gratified by the level of response, which eventually led to significant changes in some articles.[12]

This process may be viewed as a modern counterpart to the consultation at Schleitheim, where early Anabaptists forged several articles of agreement. Since confessions of faith often serve as the most visible and accessible statements of belief and practice, hermeneutic communities may serve particularly well in the formulation, discussion and final adoption of such documents.

Area or denominational groups may also function to discern God's will in regard to particular issues of moral import, resulting in the adoption of position statements. Because statements of church position generally rest on biblical values, hermeneutical discernment is often an important part of the process. For example, as a denomination particularly concerned about peacemaking, the Mennonite Church adopted a number of key statements about peace and other social concerns.[13] The formulation, discussion, and adoption of such statements often relied on group discussion and hermeneutical discernment.

Some translocal groups have the right to make binding decisions for local churches, particularly in regard to controversial issues such as ordination for women or membership privileges for persons with same-sex orientation. In the debates that generally precede such decisions, the approach to discernment and scriptural interpretation profoundly influences the discernment process.

On yet a larger level than a national denomination is the global fellowship of churches that relate to each other, whether in closely related families of faith or in vastly differing traditions. (The Mennonite World Conference and the World Council of Churches serve as an example of the two ends of this spectrum.) Because the world has become a global community, Christians must not ignore the insights of their neighbors around the globe in their interpretation of Scripture. McKenna (220) states the mandate succinctly: "Community isn't just the group we're in at the moment, the parish or church we belong to—it's more, always more. It includes believers world-wide, the universal church in other countries and continents."

Travel, telecommunications, and international exchanges make it relatively simple to engage in dialogue on matters of mutual concern. The perspectives of the world community can greatly enrich the nature of the discussion, particularly when their plight is vastly different.

Prophetic Communities

Ever since the School of the Prophets in Old Testament times, believers have coalesced into prophetic communities for mutual support on matters of concern. Seeking both to hear and speak for God, prophetic groups often confront the larger community, church, or society of which they are a part. A prophetic community may readily serve as a hermeneutic community for discernment, particularly in regard to specific issues. Several examples in the Mennonite church can illuminate the matter.

In 1957, a group of young Anabaptist scholars who studied in Europe brought together a series of conferences on issues of pacifism, church-state relationships, and ecumenical dialogue. These young intellectuals, primarily graduates of Goshen College, also published a series of pamphlets under the rubric of *Concern*.

In general, they eschewed traditional Mennonite pietism and embraced Enlightenment ideas. They goaded the institutional church and its aging leaders to find appropriate ways to exercise greater social and political responsibility.[14] By appealing to the radical nature of early Anabaptism, the writers hoped to restore the dynamism of the movement and shake off the complacency the church had acquired through years of quiet sect-hood.

As an expression of prophetic community, the *Concern* series urged the Mennonite church toward greater faithfulness to its biblical calling, as well as greater emulation of primitive Anabaptism. While the Concern movement was relatively short-lived, the writers gained places of prominence in the church, disseminating these ideas in academic institutions as well as official church publications. While the influence of the Concern movement is not easily measured, many of its ideas on pacifism and social responsibility have since been widely adopted in the church.

A generation later, Ronald Sider beckoned the Mennonite church worldwide to more deliberate involvement in issues of peace and justice. His efforts eventuated in the formation of two inter-denominational groups called Evangelicals for Social Action (ESA) and Christian Peacemaker Teams (CPT). ESA became a coalition of evangelical believers who take seriously their political responsibility. The organization produces a regular publication and organizes for political action on particular issues.

CPT now functions as a group of peacemakers who travel to trouble spots around the world. Members of CPT function in varied roles such as observers at democratic elections, recorders of human rights violations, and organizers of prayer vigils. Both ESA and CPT take seriously their prophetic role, seeking to heighten the conscience of both church and society on moral and political issues.

These examples serve to illustrate the work of prophetic communities who serve as discerning hermeneutic communities Members of these groups, of course, are mostly persons who are also members of other church communities. The drawing factor is a body of shared concerns rather than worship, fellowship, and mutual accountability as in a local church. Combining unity of conviction with the strength of numbers, they have the ability to address the conscience of the broader church. Their greatest strength, however, may also be a weakness. Without the representation of different viewpoints commonly found in local churches, such prophetic communities lack the perspectives of diversity which can greatly enrich a discernment process.

Academic Institutions/Societies

Church-related academic institutions or societies may function as hermeneutic communities, particularly in the area of scholarly biblical exegesis. Meetings of faculty as well as published papers provide the forum for hermeneutical discussion, dispute, and discernment. Traditionally, the academy emphasizes the freedom of inquiry, while the church is confessional in nature. This basic difference significantly impacts the nature of the resulting hermeneutic community. In the academic community, hermeneutical discernment values creative thought, clarity or profundity of ideas, scholarly accuracy, and citation of critical sources. With such attention given to the human dimension, there may be less emphasis on prayer, waiting on God, or the gifts of the Spirit operating the group.

Closely related to the academic community are societies formed for the purpose of Bible translation. Generally inter-denominational in membership, they bring together a community of scholars for the purpose of gaining consensus on the best wording of biblical texts. As discussed above, some theories of translation allow for the creation of modern-day equivalents to biblical situations. Free translations therefore, allow for a great freedom in the interpretation of a text.

Perhaps the most poignant example of such a community project is the production of a recent translation called *The New Living Translation*. Prompted partly by objections to the overly free style of its popular single-author *paraphrase* called the Living Bible, the Tyndale House Publishers published a *translation* produced by a group of translators. A primary difference between the two efforts is the amount of collaboration and accountability regarding the wording of the text. The Bible Translation Team for the latter includes several translators for each book of the Bible, plus reviewers and a coordinating team.

While not all of these persons may have been in the same room at the same time, the joint effort represents a significant hermeneutic goal, that of translating the Bible into modern-day speech. Surely the community functioned at times as a forum for discussion, confrontation, and correction on the meaning of Scripture passages. As such, it served as a hermeneutical community.

Virtual Communities

The advent of computer electronic communications, particularly in its expression as the Internet, has revolutionized the way people around the world communicate with each other. The ability to send and receive messages online in any number of electronic and social media now make it possible for groups to "meet" and "converse" while being physically located in diverse places around the globe. Virtual communities have sprung up for work, play, and affiliation. Along with businesses and other special interest groups, the church has joined the company of those who benefit from telecommunication.

Virtual communities can serve as one type of hermeneutical community, particularly for those participants who are committed to ongoing interaction. Because of their significant exposure, ideas shared via the Web introduce both a new kind of responsibility and accountability. Even as legal actions challenge the rights and freedoms of "hate groups" and purveyors of pornography to post their ideas, Christians must be aware of the moral responsibility for the ideas they share. While television broadcasting has long made it possible to disseminate ideas, it has not provided for a feedback loop now provided by the web. When ideas are shared via the Web, persons have the facility to respond quickly.

Thus, the Internet is a place to disseminate, test, and refine ideas to virtual communities. Telecommunications provides "high tech" and "high touch,"[15] albeit a touch of a different kind. While sociologists may well insist that it is impossible to experience true discernment within the limits of virtual community, they can help the church around the world.

SUMMARY

The vision for a discerning hermeneutic community is rooted in the nature and purpose of the church as a community called by God and redeemed by Jesus Christ. The faithful church is committed to its calling to be and make disciples of Jesus Christ. This commitment is expressed in three dimensions—worship, community, and mission. Within each of these dimensions, the church's activities are significantly shaped by biblical hermeneutics and discernment. Therefore, the discerning hermeneutic community is not simply one activity of the church, to be exercised at special times. Rather, it is a function of the church that pervades its entire corporate life and mission.

Although the local church is the primary place where Christians gather in discerning hermeneutic communities, they also exist at various other levels, both inside the church and beyond. These communities, whether short-lived or long-term, can contribute significantly to God's mission in the world.

NOTES

1. See *Congregational Discipling* for an explication of an educational model built around a three-fold vision for worship, community, and mission, with disciple-making at its core.

2. Expository sermons are considered by some to be one form of a propositional sermon. (Cf. Wilson 205-210). In this typology, expository sermons follow a particular form of idea development: 1) introduction, 2) exposition of a biblical text, 3) a bridge to our own time and situation, and 4) a conclusion which exhorts to action. Expository sermons have sometimes been highly formulaic in structure, perhaps depending on three points drawn from the text. But expository preaching need not be pedantic, abstract, or static in form. Expository sermons may employ many different forms, as long as they attempt to make clear the meaning of the scripture to the hearers and call them to response.

3. While Anabaptists favor the New Testament, many of the New Testament references to the church as God's people (cf. 1 Pet. 2:10) show that the early church drew on Old Testament concepts for much of its self-understanding (cf. Exod. 7:6, 2 Sam. 7:24).

4. Cf. Revelation 1:3.

5. Realistically, what one person experiences as a safe place may feel dangerous to another. The church often struggles, for example, with the critical insights and doubts of scholars in its midst. Consequently, the church generally needs to provide small groups that function in different ways according to one's needs. While Biblical scholars must have freedom to exercise critical thought, they must also learn to express their findings in ways (and places) that build up the discipling community.

6. See Rupp, who warns against the twin dangers of complacency and nostalgia in modern community life. Both lead the church to turn in on itself.

7. Biblical phrases or entire verses are sometimes used as a rubric to express the church's vision.

8. Mennonites share a conviction that "the church is involved in cross-cultural mission whether it reaches out to people of the majority culture, to people of minority cultures within the society, or to various cultural groups in other countries" (*Confession*, 44-5).

9. Beyond simple observation, there are systematic approaches one may helpfully use to "exegete" a social situation. One method is developed in Holland and Henriot. These authors assert that social analysis is fraught with numerous difficulties. One such difficulty is the increasing complexity of our society. Further, society is changing so rapidly that one can not readily make assumptions today based on yesterday's analysis. For these reasons, it is extremely difficult to identify cause and effect. Moral choices are often complex and controversial. It is much easier to stick to the basics and avoid the hard questions. Yet it is imper-

ative to discern the world in which we live.

10. In some contexts, house churches, intentional communities, and base communities may function as a local church, with heightened social interaction.

11. The Mennonite Church and the General Conference Mennonite Church adopted *Confession of Faith in a Mennonite Perspective* in their joint assembly at Wichita, Kansas, in July 1995.

12. Significantly, the first draft of Article 4, "Scripture," received the most feedback. The final draft of the document reflected a stronger sense of biblical authority as well as stronger statements about the divine authorship of scripture.

13. For a list of peace-related statements, see Appendices 3 and 4 in Stutzman (2011, 321-330).

14. However, John Howard Yoder (1994 163), one of the early Concern writers, believes that it is dangerous for Christians to assume "responsibility" for Christian outcomes in society. These conclusions often lead to war. He argues from a sectarian, rather than establishmentarian, point of view. Thus, he believes that the Quakers, the Methodists, and revivals along the American frontier shaped the moral tone of this nation more than Anglo-Saxon democratic traditions. "The prophetic function of the church, properly interpreted, is more effective against injustice than getting mixed in the partisan political process oneself."

15. Although a telecommunications company once advertised their phone service with the invitation to "reach out and touch someone," this is impossible in physical terms.

CHAPTER 6

·······················

CONCLUSION

SUMMARY

The purpose of this study has been to discuss how an implementation of the discernment function of free church ecclesiology can effectively aid the contemporary church in communal efforts at biblical interpretation, even amid conflict and controversy. The introductory chapter set forth this thesis, arguing that many references to the hermeneutic community were primarily ideological and not sufficiently concrete or practical really to test the concept in the life of a congregation. This study has fleshed out the concept of hermeneutic community by linking it with the discernment function of the church, and showing how discernment and interpretation take place in congregations or other church groups.

Chapter Two explored the nature of the free church as a community for discernment, including the concrete steps which discernment may take in ecclesial groups. As scholars in the free church tradition have argued, the mandate for discernment is inherent in Christ's instruction to his disciples. In the free church, discernment is a response to Christ's call to discipleship, involving not only church leaders or the elite but also every member in covenant relationship with the congregation. The shape of the communal discernment process may vary considerably, of course, depending on the size of the group and the nature of the discernment being exercised.

Chapter Three explored the practice of biblical interpretation in the Anabaptist tradition. While some of the concepts of sixteenth-century Anabaptist hermeneutics continue to be relevant today, modern developments have deeply influenced current hermeneutic practices, including differing concepts of the hermeneutic community. Revisionist social historians have questioned both the accuracy and relevance of earlier accounts of Anabaptist hermeneutic practice, arguing for a more nuanced approach than the monogenetic accounts of Anabaptist origins would have suggested or allowed. Hermeneutic emphases and practices varied both within and among various regions where Anabaptism took hold.

Even today, varying degrees of identity with Anabaptism influence hermeneutic practices. Further, the effects of modernism and accompanying individualism significantly shape the practices of communal life in the church. Community takes on various forms, including global networks not possible in an earlier era. At the same time, people live in close proximity to people they have never met, a rare phenomenon in the premodern world.

Chapter Four explored ways to work with differences, both ideological and practical, that arise in communal processes of discernment and interpretation. The discussion showed the value of a dialectic approach to both biblical/theological tensions and the practical dilemmas of ordinary life. Polarity management is an important skill to learn in group process. At the same time, there are limits to conversation; not all differences will be solved through ongoing dialogue, particularly when differing values underlie the disagreement. And sometimes difficult people participate in the process in such a way that not even modest consensus seems possible.

Chapter Five set forth a vision for discerning hermeneutic communities, building on free church commitments to discipleship expressed in worship, fellowship, and community. Discernment and interpretation are not isolated functions of the church; they are woven into the fabric of the church's essential group activities. Yet, while the worshiping congregation remains the primary exemplar for hermeneutic community, there are other forms of community that contribute both to discernment and interpretation in the larger Christian community.

This study has shown the close relationship between discernment and biblical interpretation. Both draw on the ability of the church to make assessments about its context and concrete applications of its moral axioms. Both express the corporate nature of the church, drawing on the varied gifts, perspectives, and interests in the body of Christ, and addressing its varied needs. Further, group processes of discernment and interpretation have much in common, since both rely on good facilitation and effective communication among participants. Finally, both discernment and interpretation in the free church have their foundation in a dynamic relationship with Jesus, informed by a dynamic view of Scripture.

RECOMMENDATIONS FOR FURTHER STUDY

While this study has explored the practical implications of the free church vision for discerning hermeneutic communities, much more work could fruitfully be done. On the level of research, one could study free church congregations to determine the extent to which they actually function as discerning hermeneutic communities. In this vein, one could survey both pastors and members to compare their attitudes about discernment and interpretation in the life of the church.

One could also study the relationship between theological commitments and the commitment to processes of discernment, perhaps by comparing congregations in the free church tradition with churches in a different churchly tradition.

One might also trace the changing commitments of the church on a particularly salient moral issues, such as abortion, homosexuality, or support for pacifism versus war, looking for the social processes by which the church determines its stance.

Again, one might fruitfully study congregational conflicts to see how well a polarity management approach helps congregations to deal with differences arising in discernment and hermeneutic processes.

Perhaps on the most practical level, one could develop and test a model for training congregations and their leaders in the processes of discernment and hermeneutic interpretation. One could, for example, develop a guide for groups to use in the study of specific Scripture or specific pressing issues, laying out steps for discerning the meaning and application of that particular text in the life of the church. It would ideally combine discernment and interpretation of Scripture with exegesis of the group's social milieu.

While these kinds of guides exist for individual interpretation, they are designed primarily for group discussion, such as in Sunday school or in a small group. There are fewer guides for discernment processes that are designed effectively to lead a group to make decisions or adopt a particular stance on moral issues.

Although the concept of the hermeneutic community remains an ideal in the free church, the winds of contemporary life threaten to rip the communal life of the church from its biblical roots and to fracture the bonds that make community processes possible at all. Only as churches make particular efforts to specify and concretize their theological commitments in the practices of ordinary life will they be able to stand firm in the face of life's storms. May God grant grace for that calling.

Chapter 7
....

Responses

VALUING BIBLICAL INTERPRETATION AND SUPPORT-ING COUNTER-INTUITIVE DISCERNMENT MOVES

Every community of faith has to wrestle with the understand-ing and application of biblical interpretation for faithfulness in the present moment. Ervin Stutzman is envisioning an in-creased role for congregational discernment as one of the tools of faithful hermeneutics in the Anabaptist tradition. He expli-cates the role and complexities of group discernment well and provides a treasure trove of insights and information.

Ultimately, however, the effectiveness of Listening to God in community hinges on all members' understanding experi-entially what to do with their own thoughts, feelings, notions and convictions as a well-functioning part of the body of Christ. Stutzman's study calls out for a follow-up piece that fleshes out how being a productive participant in corporate discernment is integral to faithful discipleship in the Anabaptist tradition.

Folks have very little help understanding what they are supposed to do with their cherished sense of right and wrong. So even as followers of Christ we often default to persuad-ing/being persuaded, winning/losing, fighting/splitting. The challenge of group discernment is to offer the fullness of one's perspective and giftedness as gift to God and the community *while at the same time* totally releasing that to be acted upon by the Holy Spirit in community.

This is a counter-intuitive move. It takes practice and corporate grace as we try and fail. It is both painful and joyous. It is humbling and liberating. It is the fastest spiritual formation track for discipleship I know. There is nothing that matures a congregation faster than learning to trust God's transforming power among us as we honor the Spirit of God in our brothers and sisters even when they are most certainly "wrong." Corporate discernment is not a process. It is making space for a miracle—the witness to the world that God can make something amazing with the likes of us.

It would be valuable to have the type of in-depth study Stutzman so well exemplifies developed to explicate the *construct* of personal discipleship/faithfulness required to prepare and empower folks to be helpful participants in healthy congregational life and discernment. Being committed to Christ—in and of itself—does not empower folks for the task of being disciples-in-community. Knowing that we should be part of the hermeneutical community does not mean we know how to do that helpfully. We all have to untangle from myriad of predispositions, mind sets, expectations, and experiences to migrate into a new vision of what it means to be disciples in a community of Christ.

The Anabaptist tradition has much to teach the rest of us about discipleship. We would be deeply helped by resources offering an integrated vision and construct for what this would look like and how we might function in it. Meanwhile we are privileged to be able to draw on Stutzman's highlighting of biblical interpretation in congregational contexts as one key resource on the discernment path. —*Jan Wood, Seattle, Washington, is Author (with Lon Fendall and Bruce Bishop) of* Practicing Discernment Together: Finding God's Way Forward in Decision Making *(Barclay Press, 2007); she is also Director, Good News Associates.*

DISCERNING AS A WAY TO GIVE GOD DELIGHT

In *Discerning God's Will Together*, Ervin Stutzman proposes that the contemporary church, faced with difficult decisions about moral and practical issues, can learn from the long tradition of communal discernment and biblical interpretation that goes hand-in-hand with the Anabaptist understanding of the congregation as a voluntary community of believers, committed to following Christ and, with the guidance of the Holy Spirit, together seeking to understand God's will for their particular situation.

Stutzman provides helpful background for the reader as he delves into ways free church ecclesiology shapes the role of the congregation as the locus for discernment and biblical interpretation. He reviews Anabaptist approaches to biblical interpretation, looking back to our roots as well as including insights from modern biblical, sociological, and communication studies.

Stutzman offers a good, though brief, introduction to congregational discernment; congregational leaders attempting to plan the details of a particular discernment process may want to draw on additional resources, whether trained facilitators or books such as *Grounded in God: Listening Hearts Discernment for Group Deliberations* (Farnham et al, Morehouse Publishing, 1999), *Discerning God's Will Together: A Spiritual Practice for the Church* (Morris and Olsen, Alban Publications, 1998); *Sharing Wisdom: A Process for Group Decision Making* (McKinney, Tabor Publishing, 1987); or *In Tune with God: The Art of Congregational Discernment* (Glick, Mennonite Publishing Network, 2004).

Drawing on his wealth of experience as a church leader and mediator, Stutzman goes into more depth in his discussion of healthy polarity management and conflict transformation. I found his presentation of a number of key polarities particularly helpful for better understanding the complications of our discernment conversations and the ways we often talk past each other, whether at congregational or denominational levels.

Addressing these multiple levels, Stutzman rightly points out the importance of translocal conversations for coming to a deeper and broader understanding of issues on which we disagree. He notes that some translocal groups have the right to make binding decisions for local churches, particularly in regard to controversial issues such as ordination for women or same-sex membership privileges. I would have liked to see him address the question of who and how we discern which issues qualify for such binding, since the issues have changed over time for North American Mennonites. Are they simply the hot topics of the era? Or are there other criteria for what we discern together beyond the congregation?

In his chapter on hermeneutic communities, Stutzman discusses ways discernment is woven into the congregational spheres of worship, community, and mission, and suggests a number of practices that help to form us as faithful, discerning communities. While a good start, this section could be fruitfully expanded to include areas where we stand in need of transformation, individually and communally.

For example, Stutzman names a commitment to discipleship as central to our discernment. While I fully agree, it is important also to name that our discipleship is always in response to God's love and grace. In my work as a spiritual guide for groups and individuals, I find that many of us struggle to recognize and receive God's persistent reaching out to us, falling instead into the trap of feeling we have to get our act together first, figuring out the right thing to do and doing it well, to be worthy of God's love.

Similarly, Stutzman defines discernment as "a means by which people of faith come to understand God's will for a particular situation." Again, I agree, but with the caution that the phrase *God's will* can be a stumbling block for some. We need to understand it in its full, biblical expression, not as a tightrope to be gingerly walked—but as God's plan to bring all things into right relationship, all that gives God delight and is in line with God's purposes, all that is in tune with God's song.

Given the tidal wave of information and the urgent busyness that make up most of our lives, it takes effort to discover the individual and communal practices that open us to God's transforming love, shaping and developing us as faithful followers of Christ and as communities of healing and hope. Stutzman's book will be an excellent resource for congregations wanting to make this effort, providing a good introduction to the theory and practice of the corporate practice of discernment. —*Sally Weaver Glick, Elkhart, Indiana, is Author,* In Tune with God: The Art of Congregational Discernment; *she also serves on the Leadership Enhancement Team for Indiana-Michigan Mennonite Conference.*

CONGREGATIONS MATTER

Congregations matter. As Robert D. Putnam concluded after extensive research on the decline of social groups in the United States, "Faith communities in which people worship together are arguably the single most important repository of social capital in America" (*Bowling Alone: The Collapse and Revival of American Community*, Simon and Schuster, 2000). Those of us who participate in congregational life know that they are important not only for their ability to assemble people but also for their emotional and spiritual impact on members and their communities. Yet perhaps because of their unique role in assembling diverse individuals and intervening in our lives, congregations also are often the locus of persistent social conflict.

Ervin Stutzman deals directly with this conundrum in his comprehensive and compassionate call for congregations and other Christian groups to become communities of discernment. As Stutzman asserts, "the people of God are called to be discerning as a *group* (*Discerning*, 2013, 21, emphasis added). Stutzman suggests that such discernment will require both a christocentric (Christ-centered) and an "ecclesiocentric" (church-centered) commitment. In other words, genuine Christian discernment becomes possible only as we gather as a community of believers striving to follow Jesus together in a particular time and place.

While this sounds compelling in principle, Stutzman acknowledges the multiple challenges of accomplishing such discernment in practice. Part of the challenge comes from our history, as congregations and associations that emerged from the Anabaptist movement received an "extremely sectarian" heritage (*Discerning*, 45). The emphasis on theological correctness and purity of practice produced an "urge to purge" that resulted in a fragmented movement.

But our challenges are not only historical. Mennonites and Brethren have not been immune to modernization pressures, and both higher education and urbanization have produced dramatic variations on the monocultural rural communities they once inhabited. Recent societal polarization (focused on issues such as abortion, "gay marriage," gun ownership, and the role of government) has also divided many congregations and associations.

Amid such difference, how then can we discern together? Stutzman is clear in response. We must affirm our core convictions—beginning with following Jesus, including the Anabaptist distinctives of simplicity, community, and peace. And we must learn to embrace paradox and the disciplines of good process. This triad of affirming shared beliefs and values, embracing paradox, and practicing good process will indeed permit genuine community discernment in the great majority of situations and issues. But Stutzman himself admits it may not be adequate in high intensity conflict. What then?

I would agree that in situations of high intensity "intractable" conflict, such as we are now experiencing regarding participation of LGBT (lesbian, gay, bisexual, transexual) individuals in the life and leadership of the church, the excellent discernment model Stutzman offers will not be adequate. Instead of relying solely on our embrace of paradox and good process, we will need to reaffirm our *polity*. If the congregation and the conference (as clusters of congregations are called in Mennonite Church USA) are seen as the core locus of discernment, and if differing congregations and conferences are permitted to reach differing conclusions regarding the level of participation of LGBT members, then I can envision a way forward. If instead a denomination such as MC USA insists on a purity and uniformity narrative that demands denominational conformity from all, we are headed toward inevitable schism.

Here I am deeply grateful not only to Anabaptist core beliefs (such as simplicity, community, and peace) but to core Anabaptist polity. We do not seek theological or ecclesiological experts who prescribe what we must all believe and practice. Rather, we look to our gathered communities to discern together, in the light of Scripture and the illumination of the Holy Spirit, what God is calling our community to become. This is not "rugged individualism" as it is predicated on the model of a discerning community rather than an isolated individual. It is, instead, a return to the pre-Constantinian model of Acts 6 and Acts 15, where a local community could discern how to respond to needy widows and a larger association could permit differing entry requirements for two different ethno-religious groups (Jews and Gentiles).

While the Constantinian model of Christianity requires an assembled hierarchy and sameness of belief and practice, the early church and the Anabaptist movement both embraced local expressions and diversity of practice. Genuine discernment in the future will require not only the theology and tools that Stutzman carefully develops but also a firm rejection of Constantinian models of monolithic decision-making. —*David Brubaker, Associate Professor of Organizational Studies at the Center for Justice and Peacebuilding, Eastern Mennonite University*

THE AUTHOR RESPONDS TO RESPONDENTS

My first and fundamental response to all three of the above respondents is "Yes, you've grasped the essence of what I've tried to do in this study and you've offered some perceptive suggestions to compensate for its limitations." I am grateful for both their affirmations and their suggestions for strengthening the church's corporate practice of discernment. They deserve a few words of response to their suggestions.

In this book, I set out to explore the theological and biblical mandate for congregational discernment, particularly as understood by the free church. As biblical literacy fades in church as well as society, we need to be reminded of the biblical and theological foundations of our beliefs and ethics. From my long experience as a church leader, I am painfully aware that for many of us, our practice of corporate discernment lags far behind the theological and historical declarations printed in our confessions of faith and church statements. Many congregations have only one corporate gathering per week, and the average member attends only one-half to one-third of those meetings. That level of corporate interaction is hardly sufficient engagement for meaningful group discernment.

Therefore, as Jan Wood helpfully points out, church members need an orientation to what it means to be a faithful disciple of Jesus amid other disciples who have radically different notions of right and wrong. Or, in her words, we need an explication of "the *construct* [emphasis hers] of personal discipleship/faithfulness required to prepare and empower folks to be helpful participants in healthy congregational life and discernment." I agree with what I take to be her basic premise— that one must learn to be a discerning person on the individual level before one can enter meaningfully into corporate discernment. Further, I believe that individual disciples must practice the classic spiritual disciplines to participate meaningfully in a corporate process designed to hear God's will for a group.

In the same vein, I concur with Sally Weaver Glick's assertion that we "name that our discipleship is always in response to God's love and grace." How true! Through my own experience of spiritual guidance, I have come to see that much of my life of discipleship unfolds in response the many-hued forms of God's grace. More than just a way to salvation, grace is expressed in all the ways God helps us carry the burdens that come with being human—forgiveness of sins, transformation of character and habits into the likeness of Jesus Christ, the empowerment and gifts of the Holy Spirit, wisdom for making decisions, the encouragement from others in the body of Christ, the "gracelets" that fall on the worshipping assembly— these are but a few expressions of God's manifold love.

Wood also helpfully points out the need to offer "the fullness of one's perspective and giftedness as gift to God and the community *while at the same time* [emphasis hers] totally releasing that to be acted upon by the Holy Spirit in community." I take her comments to reflect the Quaker practice of "shedding"—seeking to rid oneself of biases, inordinate attachments, or grudges that would skew our perceptions of others or compromise our ability to listen attentively to viewpoints that differ from our own. Again, Quakers seek for the ideal of "indifference" to anything but that which is of God.

Perhaps the best biblical example of shedding or indifference is that of Jesus Christ in the Garden of Gethsemane, praying "Father, if you are willing, take this cup from me; yet not my will, but yours be done" (Luke 22:42 NIV). The Anabaptists spoke of *Gelassenheit*, or willingness to yield to the group, a trait emphasized much more strongly among the Amish than in most modern Mennonite contexts. Among the latter, we seek to honor social "prophets" who take a lonely and/or costly stand for the right. These differing values can lead to deep tension in our attempts to discern God's will as a group.

Wood also makes the point that process itself will not lead to corporate discernment unless it makes "space for a miracle—the witness to the world that God can make something amazing with the likes of us." I agree, since I have the assurance that process matters to her as much as it does to me. In the book cited at the end of her response, Wood and co-authors Lon Fendall and Bruce Bishop offer several checklists which outline a process to follow in discernment. While process alone will never bring good discernment, a lack of good process can practically forestall it. I heartily affirm what I take Wood to be saying; the goal of a discernment process lies beyond the reach of merely human endeavor. God is the main actor from start to finish, calling us to a place of understanding made possible by the presence of the Holy Spirit in our midst. That is why the conference in Acts 15 reported that "It seemed good to the Holy Spirit and to us. . ." (Acts 15:28).

Further, in processes of group discernment, I have observed that we often find it difficult to "shed" biases or preconceived notions not simply for personal reasons but also due to deeply held values or beliefs embraced by our group. This prevents our being "indifferent." Rather, we see the only right disposition in the discernment process as being to stake out and defend a position on the basis of conscience—like Luther before the Diet of Worms: "Here I stand, I can do no other. God help me. Amen." For some of us, the value is holiness or purity. For others, the value is justice. As I have attempted to show in this study, corporate discernment requires the ability to hold even our most important values in tension with each other. So, as Wood observes, we need both instruction and practice in what to do with our "cherished sense of right and wrong."

In her response, Sally Weaver Glick points out that "congregational leaders attempting to plan the details of a particular discernment process may want to draw on additional resources" and then goes on to recommend several of them. Although I am not familiar with all of the resources she cites, I fully agree that specific training in group discernment process is not only helpful but perhaps even essential in many contexts. I long for the day when we have a cadre of trained and Spirit-led "discernmentarians" who can guide congregations through shoals which can easily lead to shipwreck.

Glick also voices the wish that I might "address the question of who and how we discern which issues qualify" for translocal binding, "since the issues have changed over time for North American Mennonites." I confess that I find this question to be one of the most difficult ones to address in my church leadership role. The recent acceleration of social change and the deep assimilation of the Mennonite church into modern society have led to widespread disregard for translocal authority on almost any level, including that of the denomination. As Brubaker points out, modern Mennonites and Brethren have followed societal trends that have led to deep polarization on issues such as "abortion, 'gay marriage,' gun ownership, and the role of government." I recently heard a Brethren denominational leader tell annual meeting delegates that he's not sure he can find "one square inch" of common ground in the denomination. At times, I feel I could say the same for Mennonite Church USA.

In this vein, I find David Brubaker's critique and suggestions to be helpful. The free church which is the subject of this study is meant, after all, to be a *free* church. That means it is free to determine its best associations and to decide via associative covenants whether or not it will be bound by translocal rules. Mennonite Church USA, for example, grants freedom for congregations to determine the criteria by which members can join the congregation, it grants freedom for area conferences to determine the criteria by which congregations can belong to the conference, and it grants freedom for the denomination to determine the criteria by which area conferences can join the denomination. At every level, individuals or groups may choose to leave the "parent group." I say it somewhat tongue in cheek, but I find it to be largely true: many congregations would like the denomination to enforce translocal rules on groups that differ from their convictions and practices but relax the rules that would bind their own fellowship.

In recent years people in one "camp" have urged Mennonite Church USA to sign prophetic statements on such social issues as immigration, the role of women, the need for gun control, advancement of social health care, and limiting the use of military torture or drone warfare. People from a different "camp" have voiced longing for churchwide stances/statements on birth control and/or abortion, reaffirmation of biblical/traditional understandings of human sexuality and marriage, and a condemnation of Obamacare's initiatives to force businesses to fund abortions for employees. Given that dynamic, it is quite difficult to make a churchwide decision on what should be binding beyond the congregation. As I watch "hot button" topics come to the surface, I fear that our congregations are often more deeply influenced by popular media or discussion with friends than by any process of biblical/communal discernment. Given such dynamics, I agree with Brubaker's assessment that we must hew closely to our churchwide polity, which gives considerable latitude to local groups.

Nevertheless, as executive director of a denomination, I cannot with integrity speak *for the denomination* unless I align myself with statements the church has made through a process of delegate discernment assemblies. These are not hierarchical assemblies reflecting a Constantinian model of monolithic decision-making but a widely representative gathering of delegates from both local (congregational) and translocal (area conference or constituent) groups. Although these corporate statements at times reflect the work of a small advocacy group, and/or they were adopted via a process that in my judgment lacked adequate discernment, they stand as the best corporate expression of our discernment on particular social matters.

Often these statements are not intended to be *binding* on any groups but to give them guidance. In recent years, Mennonite Church USA has used "teaching position" to refer to guidance regarding human sexuality. Yet some have used this guidance as a rule to be enforced beyond the local church, to the point of expelling congregations from an area conference.

Although I have not mentioned it in the study, I have often relied on the insights of family systems theory while working through congregational discernment processes. Ed Friedman and others have helpfully pointed out that reactive *emotional processes* often trump group values or established mores in the heat of group conflict. At times, the pressure to conform to group standards can suppress the most creative insights offered by individuals. While only a theory, I believe that the insights of family systems can help group leaders understand and helpfully respond to the otherwise inexplicable reactions that can wreck a group discernment process.

As Shenk points out in her Foreword to this book, it was written primarily in a context of a white academic culture. In my recent work with discernment processes that include various racial/ethnic groups, I have come to see the need for some cultural nuances or adjustments in both the assumptions and the processes outlined in this study. At the risk of stereotyping, I will state what I have observed in Mennonite Church USA. Particularly in the Hispanic, African-American, and Asian traditions, the pastor of the church is given primary responsibility to discern and declare the will of God for the group. As one Hispanic conference leader recently said it, the better the pastor is doing, the less discernment is needed on the part of the church. If the church must be called together for group discernment for much beyond an affirmation of the pastor's plans, it signals trouble in the camp.

On the other hand, the Native American community has developed group discernment processes built on many of the same assumptions voiced in this study, and such practices mirror some of the older Anabaptist-Mennonite assumptions about humility and suppressing individual giftedness or initiatives in favor of corporate discernment. Leaders nearly always emerge through the call of the group, and they speak on behalf of the group only after a careful process of listening to group members without interruption. The "talking stick" that is often used in modern group sharing processes has deep roots in the indigenous community. Many contemporary Mennonites and Brethren have much to learn from them.

In sum, the responses from Wood, Glick, and Brubaker, as well as Shenk, point to a need for further work in several different areas that have not been adequately addressed in this book. While I have addressed their suggestions only briefly here, I have been inspired to keep working on these ideas in other contexts. I dream of others who, after reading this study, will be similarly motivated to help the free church build on its good tradition of biblical/communal discernment and to discover dimensions of God's grace in our corporate life that we have not yet imagined. —*Ervin R. Stutzman*

....

Sources Cited

ARTICLES AND ESSAYS

Bender, Harold S. "The Anabaptist Theology of Discipleship." *Concern*, No. 18, July 1971, 36-44.

———. The Anabaptist Vision. *Mennonite Quarterly Review (MQR)* 17 (April 1944): 67-88.

"Biblical Interpretation in the Life of the Church," Mennonite Church General Assembly, June 18-24, 1977, Estes Park, Col. Appendix I in *Slavery, Sabbath, War, and Women*, Willard M. Swartley.

Burkholder, J. Lawrence. "The Church as a Discerning Community." *Gospel Herald* 58.6, 1965, 113.

———. "The Peace Churches as Communities of Discernment." *Christian Century* 80, Sept. 4, 1963, 1072-1075.

"A Christian Declaration on the Authority of the Scriptures." General Conference Mennonite Church, Bethlehem, Pa. Newton, Kan.: Faith and Life Press, 1962.

Dietterich, Inagrace T. "Cultivating Missional Communities: The Bible." *The Center Letter* 26.12 (1996): 1-2.

Dintaman, Steve. "The Pastoral Significance of the Anabaptist Vision." In *Refocusing a Vision: Shaping Anabaptist Character in the Twenty-First Century*, ed. John D. Roth. Goshen, Ind.: Mennonite Historical Society, 1995, 35-50.

Ewert, David. "The Covenant Community and Mission." In *Consultation on Anabaptist Mennonite Theology*, ed. A. J. Klassen. Fresno: Council of Mennonite Seminaries, 127-147.

Grudem, Wayne. "Do Inclusive Language Bibles Distort Scripture? Yes." *Christianity Today* 41.12, 1997, 26-32.

Harder, Lydia. "Hermeneutic Community—A Feminist Challenge." In *Perspectives on Feminist Hermeneutic*, ed. Gayle G. Koontz and Willard M. Swartley. Elkhart, Ind.: Institute for Mennonite Studies, 1987, 46-55.

Hyde, Michael J., and Craig R. Smith. "Hermeneutics and Rhetoric: A Seen but Unobserved Relationship." *The Quarterly Journal of Speech* 65 (1979): 347-63.

Jacobsen, Douglas. "Unpacking 'Inclusivity': Inclusive and Discerning?" *Christian Century* 116, 1999, 440-2.

Kouns, Eric A. "What Kind of a Book is the Bible?" *EAF Newsletter* 1, 1994, 1-4.

Krahn, Cornelius "Menno and Discipleship." *Studies in Church Discipline*. Newton, Kan.: Mennonite Publication Office, 1958, 63-80.

Kuiper, Frits. "The Pre-eminence of the Bible in Mennonite History." In *Essays in Biblical Interpretation*, ed. Willard M. Swartley. Elkhart, Ind.: Institute for Mennonite Studies, 1984, 115-30.

Kniss, Philip L. "The Authority of the Bible and the Authority of the Faith Community." In ADCP booket for Eastern Mennonite University, 1994.

Litfin, Duane A. "The Perils of Persuasive Preaching." *Christianity Today* 21.9, 1977, 14.

Littell, Franklin H. "The Work of the Holy Spirit in Group Decisions," *MQR* 34 (1960): 75-96.

McGrath, M. Burt. "A Hermeneutics of Community and Obedience: Anabaptist-Mennonite Biblical Interpretation." Unpublished paper written for Werner Jeanrod at Trinity College for the course in Hermeneutics and Theological Method, 1993.

Miller, Levi. "A Reconstruction of Evangelical Anabaptism." In *Refocusing a Vision: Shaping Anabaptist Character in the Twenty-First Century*, ed. John D. Roth. Goshen, Ind.: Mennonite Historical Society, 1995, 23-34.

Osborne, Grant R. "Do Inclusive Language Bibles Distort Scripture? No." *Christianity Today* 41.12, 1997, 33-38.

Roth, John D. "Living Between the Times: 'The Anabaptist Vision and Mennonite Reality' Revisited." In *Refocusing a Vision:*

Shaping Anabaptist Character in the Twenty-First Century, ed. John D. Roth. Goshen, Ind.: Mennonite Historical Society, 1995, 51-63.

———. "Community as Conversation: A New Model of Anabaptist Hermeneutics." In *Essays in Anabaptist Theology*, ed. H. Wayne Pipkin. Elkhart, Ind.: Institute of Mennonite Studies, 1994, 35-50.

Roth, Roy D. "The Two Kingdoms." *Gospel Herald* 48, February 1, 1955, 97-98.

Ruth, John L. "Where Shall We Go for wWsdom?" *Gospel Herald* 85 August 4, 1992, 1-3.

Sawatsky, Rodney J. " The Quest for a Mennonite Hermeneutic." *Conrad Grebel Review* 11.1 (1993): 1-20.

Schemel, George J. and Judith A. Roemer. "Communal Discernment." *Pamphlet* with revised text (1992) from *Religious* 40.6 (1981).

Schroeder, David. "Biblical Interpretation." In *Perspectives on Feminist Hermeneutics*, ed. Gail Gerber Koontz and Willard Swartley. Elkhart, Ind.: Institute for Mennonite Studies, 1987, 16-9.

———. "Discerning What is Bound in Heaven: Loosing and Binding." In *The Bible and the Church: Essays in Honor of Dr. David Ewert*, ed. A. J. Dueck, H. J. Giesbrecht, and V. G. Shillington. Winnipeg, Man.: Kindred Press, 1988, 65-73.

Scult, Allen. "The Relationship Between Rhetoric and Hermeneutics Reconsidered." *Central States Speech Journal* 34 (1983): 221-8.

Shantz, Douglas H. "The Ecclesiological Focus of Dirk Phillips' Hermeneutical Thought in 1559: a Contextual Study." In *Essays in Anabaptist Theology*, ed. H. Wayne Pipkin. Elkhart, Ind.: Institute of Mennonite Studies, 1984, 97-210.

Smucker, Marcus G. "Facing Difficult Issues: Moral and Spiritual Discernment in Congregational Decision Making." Unpublished paper. July, 1995.

Swartley, Willard M. "The Anabaptist Use of Scripture: Contemporary Applications and Prospects." In *Anabaptist Currents: History in Conversation with the Present*, ed. Bowman, Carl F. and Stephen Longenecker. Bridgewater, Va.: Penobscot Press, 1995, 65-75.

———. "Continuity and Change in Anabaptist-Mennonite Interpretation." In *Essays in Biblical Interpretation*, ed. Willard Swartley, Elkhart, Ind.: Institute of Mennonite Studies, 1984, 326-31.

Sweet, Leonard. "Can You Hear the Double Rings?" n.d.

Thomas, Robert L. "Dynamic Equivalence: A Method of Translation or a System of Hermeneutics?" http//www.mastersem.edu/journal/j1th21.htm

Toews, Paul. "Fundamentalist Conflict in Mennonite colleges: A Response to Cultural Transitions?" *MQR* 57 (July 1983): 241-56.

———. "Mennonites in American Society: Modernity and the Persistence of Religious Community." *MQR* 63 (July 1989): 227-46.

Turner, Philip. "Episcopal Authority in a Divided Church: On the Crisis of Anglican Authority." *Pro Ecclesia* (1999): 8, 23-50.

Voolstra, Sjouke. "'The Colony of Heaven': The Anabaptist Aspiration to be a Church Without Spot or Wrinkle in the Sixteenth and Seventeenth Centuries." *From Martyr to Muppy: A historical Introduction to Cultural Assimilation Processes of a Religious Minority in the Netherlands: the Mennonites.* Amsterdam: Amsterdam University Press, 1994, 15-29.

Warner, Martin, ed. "Introduction." *The Bible As Rhetoric: Studies in Biblical Persuasion and Credibility.* Warwick Studies in Philosophy and Literature. New York: Routledge. 1990.

Yancey, Philip. "Can Evangelicals Survive their Newfound Power" *Christianity Today* 27.17, 1983, 92.

Yoder, John Howard. "The Anabaptist Dissent: The Logic of the Place of the Disciple in Society." *Concern* No. 1 (1954): 45-68.

———. "Anabaptist Vision and Mennonite Reality." In *Consultation on Anabaptist Mennonite Theology*, ed. A. J. Klassen. Fresno: Council of Mennonite Seminaries, 1970, 1-46.

———. "Binding and Loosing, *Concern* No. 14, Feb 1967, 2.

Zoba, Wendy Murray. "Your Sins Shall be as White as Yucca." *Christianity Today* 41.12, 1997, 19-25.

BOOK-LENGTH WORKS

Ammerman, Nancy Tatom. *Baptist Battles: Social Change and Religious Conflict in the Southern Baptist Convention.* New Brunswick: Rutgers University Press, 1990.

Augsburger, Myron S. *Principles of Biblical Interpretation in Mennonite Theology.* Scottdale, Pa.: Herald Press, 1967.

Barton, Ruth Haley. *Pursuing God's Will Together: A Discernment Practice for Leadership Groups.* Westmont, Ill.: InterVarsity Press, 2012.

Bellah, Robert N., et. al. *Habits of the Heart.* Berkeley: University of California Press, 1985.

Bender, Harold. *These Are My People,* Scottdale, Pa.: Herald Press, 1962.

Bender, Ross T. *The People of God: A Mennonite Interpretation of the Free Church Tradition.* Scottdale, Pa.: Herald Press, 1971.

Berger, Peter L., and Thomas Luckman. *The Social Construction of Reality: A Treatise on the Sociology of Knowledge.* Garden City, N. J.: Anchor Books, 1967.

Billig, Michael. *Arguing and Thinking: A Rhetorical Approach to Social Psychology.* Cambridge: Cambridge University Press, 1987.

Boff, Leonardo. *Church: Charism and Power: Liberation Theology and the Institutional Church.* Trans. John W. Diercksmeier. New York: Crossroad, 1985.

Bossart, Donald. *Creative Conflict in Religious Education and Church Administration.* Birmingham: Religious Education Press, 1980.

Brueggemann, Walter. *Texts Under Negotiation: The Bible and Postmodern Imagination.* Minneapolis: Fortress Press, 1993.

Brunk, George R. *Ready Scriptural Reasons,* 3rd. ed. Harrisonburg, Va.: Sword and Trumpet, 1967.

Burke, Kenneth. *The Rhetoric of Religion: Studies in Logology.* Berkeley and Los Angeles: University of California Press, 1970.

Buzzard, Lynn R., and Laurence Eck. *Tell it to the Church.* Elgin: David C. Cook Publishing Co, 1982.

Confession of Faith in a Mennonite Perspective. The General Board of the General Conference Mennonite Church and the Mennonite Church General Board. Scottdale, Pa.: Herald Press, 1995.

Congregational Discipling. Mennonite Board of Congregational Ministries and Commission on Education. Scottdale, Pa.: Herald Press, 1997.

Dale, Robert. *Surviving Difficult Church Members.* Nashville: Abingdon Press, 1984.

Dietterich, Inagrace. *Gathered Together to Seek and Do God's Will.* Chicago: The Center for Parish Development, 1988.

Driver, John. *Images of the Church in Mission.* Scottdale, Pa.: Herald Press, 1997.

———. *Community and Commitment.* Scottdale, Pa.: Herald Press, 1976.

Esau, John. A., ed. *Understanding Ministerial Leadership: Essays Contributing to a Developing Theology of Ministry.* Elkhart, Ind.: Institute of Mennonite Studies, 1995.

Fendall, Lon, Jan Wood, and Bruce Bishop. *Practicing Discernment Together: Finding God's Way Forward in Decision Making.* Newberg, Ore.: Barclay Press, 2007.

Finger, Thomas N. *Christian Theology: An Eschatological Approach.* Vols. 1 and 2. Herald Press, 1985 and 1989.

Friedmann, Robert. 1973. *The Theology of Anabaptism.* Scottdale, Pa.: Herald Press.

Glick, Sally Weaver. *In Tune with God: The Art of Congregational Discernment.* Scottdale, Pa.: Faith and Life Resources, 2004.

Gresham, Charles R. *Preach the Word!* Joplin: College Press Publishing Company, 1983.

Harder, Lydia Neufeld. "Hermeneutic Community: A Study of the Contemporary Relevance of an Anabaptist-Mennonite Approach to Biblical Interpretation." Thesis. Newman Theological College, 1984.

———. *Obedience, Suspicion, and the Gospel of Mark: A Mennonite-Feminist Exploration of Biblical Authority.* Waterloo, Ont.: Wilfrid Laurier University Press, 1998.

Herberg, Will. *Protestant, Catholic, Jew: An Essay in American Religious Sociology.* Garden City, N. J.: Anchor Books, 1960.

Haugk, Kenneth C. *Antagonists in the Church.* Minneapolis: Augsburg Publishing House, 1988.

Holland, Joe and Peter Henriot. *Social Analysis: Linking Faith and Justice.* Maryknoll, N.Y.: Orbis, 1983.

Hunter, James. *American Evangelicalism: Conservative Religion and the Quandary of Modernity.* New Brunswick: Rutgers University Press, 1983.

———. *Evangelicalism: The Coming Generation.* Chicago: University of Chicago Press. 1987.

Johnson, Barry. *Polarity Management: Identifying and Managing Unsolvable Problems.* Amherst: HRD Press, 1992.

Johnson, Luke Timothy. *Decision-Making in the Church: a Biblical Model.* Minneapolis: Fortress Press, 1983.

———. *Scripture and Discernment: Decision-Making in the Church.* Nashville: Abingdon Press, 1996.

Kauffman, J. Howard, and Leo Driedger. *The Mennonite Mosaic: Identity and Modernization.* Scottdale, Pa.: Herald Press, 1991.

Kauffman, Richard A, and Gayle Gerber Koontz. *Theology for the Church: Writings by Marlin Miller.* Elkhart, Ind.: Institute of Mennonite Studies, 1997.

Klaassen, Walter, Ed. *Anabaptism in Outline: Selected Primary Sources.* Classics of the Radical Reformation, vol. 3. Scottdale, Pa.: Herald Press, 1981.

Klassen, William and Graydon F. Snyder. *Current Issues in New Testament Interpretation.* New York: Harper and Brothers, 1962.

Klein, William W., Craig Blomberg, and Robert L. Hubbard. *Introduction to Biblical Interpretation.* Dallas: Word Publishing, 1993.

Krahn, Cornelius. *Dutch Anabaptism: Origin, Spread, Life, and Thought.* Scottdale, Pa.: Herald Press, 1981.

Kraus, C. Norman. *The Community of the Spirit.* Scottdale, Pa.: Herald Press, 1993.

Kraybill, Ronald. *Repairing the Breach: Ministering in Community Conflict.* Scottdale, Pa.: Herald Press, 1981.

Leas, Speed B. *Leadership and Conflict.* Nashville: Abingdon, 1982.

———. *Moving Your Church Through Conflict.* Washington, D.C.: Alban Institute, 1985.

———. *"Should the Pastor be Fired?": How to Deal Constructively with Clergy-lay Conflict.* Washington D.C.: Alban Institute, 1980.

———. *Church Fights: Managing Conflict in the Local Church.* Philadelphia: Westminster Press, 1973.

Lederach, Paul M. *A Third Way,* Scottdale, Pa.: Herald Press, 1980.

Lindsell, Harold. *The Battle for the Bible.* Grand Rapids: Zondervan, 1976.

Littell, Franklin H. *The Origins of Sectarian Protestantism,* New York: The Macmillan Company, 1964.

McKenna, Megan. *Not Counting Women and Children: Neglected Stories from the Bible,* Maryknoll, N.Y.: Orbis, 1994.

McSwain, Larry L., and William Treadwell Jr. *Conflict Ministry in the Church.* Nashville: Broadman Press, 1981.

Miller, Marlin E. "Criticism and Analogy." *Essays on Biblical Interpretation: Anabaptist-Mennonite Perspectives.* Elkhart, Ind.: Institute of Mennonite Studies, 1984, 223-36.

Mitchell, Kenneth R. *Multiple Staff Ministries.* Philadelphia: Westminster Press, 1988.

Morris, Danny E. and Charles M. Olsen. *Discerning God's Will Together.* Washington, D.C.: Alban Publications, 1997.

Murray, Stuart Wood. *Biblical Interpretation in the Anabaptist Tradition.* Kitchener, Ont.: Pandora Press, 2000.

———. *The Naked Anabaptist: The Bare Essentials of a Radical Faith.* Scottdale, Pa.: Herald Press, 2010.

———. "Spirit, Discipleship, and Community." Ph.D. diss. Whiteford Institute, 1992.

Oswald, Roy M. and Barry Johnson. *Managing Polarities in Congregations: Eight Keys for Thriving Faith Commuities.* Herndon, Va.: The Alban Institute, 2010.

Patrick, Dale and Allen Scult. *Rhetoric and Biblical Interpretation.* Sheffield, England: Almond Press, 1990.

Pastor-Growing—People-Growing: A Manual for Leaders Who Provide Oversight for Pastors and Congregations. Elkhart, Ind.: Pastorate Project, 1995.

Redekop, Calvin. *The Free Church and Seductive Culture.* Scottdale, Pa.: Herald Press, 1970.

Robinson, Haddon. *Biblical Preaching: The Development and Delivery of Expository Messages.* Grand Rapids, Mich.: Baker Book House, 1980.

Rupp, George. *Commitment and Community.* Minneapolis: Fortress Press, 1989.

Shank, J. Ward. *The View from Round Hill,* ed. Paul L. Kratz. Harrisonburg, Va.: The Sword and Trumpet, 1988.

Shawchuck, Norman. *How to Manage Conflict in the Church: Understanding and Managing Conflict.* Vol. I. Indianapolis: Spiritual Growth Resources, 1983.

Shelley, Marshall. *Well-Intentioned Dragons: Ministering to Problem People in the Church.* Waco: Word Books, 1985.

Simons, Herbert W., Elizabeth W. Mechling, and Howard N. Schreier. "The Functions of Human Communication in Mobilizing for Action from the Bottom up: The Rhetoric of Social Movements." In *Handbook of Rhetorical and Communication Theory,* ed. Carroll C. Arnold and John Waite Bowers, 792-867. Boston: Allyn and Bacon, Inc. 1984.

Smart, James D. *The Strange Silence of the Bible in the Church.* Philadelphia: The Westminster Press, 1970.

Snodgrass, Klyne. *Between Two Truths: Living with Biblical Tensions.* Grand Rapids: Zondervan, 1990.

Snyder, C. Arnold. *Anabaptist History and Theology.* Kitchener, Ont.: Pandora Press and Scottdale, Pa.: Herald Press, 1995.

Sprunger, Mary S. "Rich Mennonites, Poor Mennonites: Economics and Theology in the Amsterdam Waterlander Congregation During the Golden Age." Diss. Uuniversity of Illinois, 1993.

Stutzman, Ervin R. "From Nonresistance to Peace and Justice: Mennonite Peace Rhetoric, 1951-1991." Diss. Temple University, 1993.

———. *From Nonresistance to Justice: The Transformation of Mennonite Church Peace Rhetoric, 1908-2008*, Studies in Anabaptist and Mennonite History, vol. 46. Scottdale, Pa.: Herald Press, 2011.

Swartley, Willard M. *Slavery, Sabbath, War, and Women: Case Studies in Biblical Interpretation*. Scottdale, Pa.: Herald Press, 1982.

———, ed. *Essays on Biblical Interpretation: Anabaptist-Mennonite Perspectives*, Elkhart, Ind.: Institute of Mennonite Studies, 1984.

——— and Gail Gerber Koontz, eds. *Perspectives on Feminist Hermeneutics*. Elkhart, Ind.: Institute of Mennonite Studies, 1987.

Trible, Phyllis. *Rhetorical Criticism: Context, Method, and the Book of Jonah*. Old Testament Series, ed. Gene M. Tucker. Minneapolis: Fortress, 1994.

Walton, Robert C. *Chronological and Background Charts of Church History*. Grand Rapids: Zondervan, 1986.

Wardlaw, Don M. *Preaching Biblically: Creating Sermons in the Shape of Scripture*. The Westminster Press, 1983.

Watson, David. *Called and Committed*. Wheaton, Ill.: Harold Shaw Publishers, 1982.

Weaver, J. Denny. *Becoming Anabaptist: The Origin and Significance of Sixteenth-Century Anabaptism*. Scottdale, Pa.: Herald Press, 1987.

Wilson, Paul Scott. *The Practice of Preaching*. Nashville: Abingdon, 1995.

Wink, Walter A. *Transforming Bible Study*, 2nd. ed. Nashville: Abingdon Press, 1989.

Witten, Marsha Grace. "'Guarding the Castle of God'—religious speech in the context of secularity: An examination of the sermon discourse of two Protestant denominations in the contemporary U.S." Diss. Princeton University, 1992.

Wuthnow, Robert. *Communities of Discourse: Ideology and Social Structure in the Reformation, the Enlightenment, and European Socialism*. Cambridge: Harvard University Press, 1989.

―――. *The Restructuring of American Religion: Society and Faith Since World War II.* Princeton: Princeton University Press, 1988.

―――. *The Struggle for America's Soul: Evangelicals, Liberals, and Secularism.* Grand Rapids: Wm B. Eerdmans Pub. Co., 1989.

Yoder, Perry. *From Word to Life: A Guide to the Art of Bible Study.* Scottdale, Pa.: Herald Press, 1982.

Yoder, John Howard. *The Fullness of Christ,* Elgin, Ill.: Brethren Press, 1987.

―――. *The Priestly Kingdom: Social Ethics as Gospel.* Notre Dame: University of Notre Dame Press, 1984.

―――. *The Royal Priesthood.* Grand Rapids: William B. Eerdmans Pub. Co., 1994.

Zehr, Paul M. *Biblical Criticism in the Life of the Church.* Scottdale, Pa.: Herald Press, 1986.

··························

The Author

*E*RVIN R. STUTZMAN IS EXECUTIVE DIRECTOR of Mennonite Church USA. He came to this role after having served for nearly a decade as Vice President for Eastern Mennonite University and Dean and Professor of Church Ministries at Eastern Mennon ite Seminary. From 2001 to 2003 he served as the moderator for Mennonite Church USA. He has also served the Mennonite Church in the roles of pastor, district overseer, and conference moderator. He received his PhD from Temple University and holds master's degrees from the University of Cincinnati and Eastern Mennonite Seminary along with a bachelor's degree from Cincinnati Christian University.

Ervin was born into an Amish home in Kalona, Iowa. After his father's death a few years later, his mother moved her family to her home community in Hutchinson, Kansas. Ervin was baptized in the Center Amish Mennonite Church near Partridge, Kansas. Later, he joined the Yoder Mennonite Church, near Yoder, Kansas. Ervin married Bonita Haldeman of Manheim, Pennsylvania. Together they served for five years with Rosedale Mennonite Missions in Cincinnati, Ohio. There Ervin was co-pastor of Mennonite Christian Assembly.

In 1982, he moved with his young family to Lancaster, Pennsylvania, to serve with Eastern Mennonite Board of Missions. He served as pastor of Mount Joy Mennonite Church before being ordained in 1984 as bishop of the Landisville District of the Lancaster Mennonite Conference. He was moderator of the conference from 1991 to 2000, when he moved to Harrisonburg, Virginia, to serve in his most recent roles.

Ervin is a preacher, a teacher, and a writer. His publications include *Creating Communities of the Kingdom* (Herald Press, 1988, co-authored with David W. Shenk); *Welcome!*, a book encouraging the church to welcome new members (Herald Press, 1990); *Being God's People*, a study for new believers (Faith & Life Resources, 1998); *Tobias of the Amish*, a story of his father's life and community (Herald Press, 2001); *Emma, A Widow Among the Amish*, the story of his widowed mother (Herald Press, 2007); and *From Nonresistance to Justice: the Transformation of Mennonite Church Peace Rhetoric, 1908-2008* (Herald Press, 2011).

Ervin enjoys doing woodworking projects in partnership with Bonita. They have three adult children, Emma, Daniel, and Benjamin and two grandchildren.

CPSIA information can be obtained at www.ICGtesting.com
Printed in the USA
BVOW020747190213

313645BV00001B/8/P